WEEDS DON'T PERISH

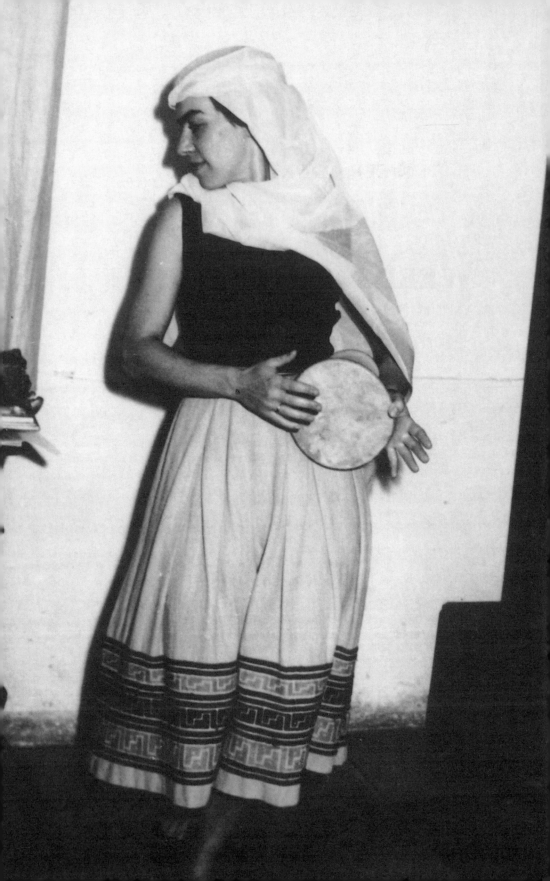

WEEDS DON'T PERISH

Memoirs of a Defiant Old Woman

HANNA BRAUN

Garnet
PUBLISHING

Weeds Don't Perish
Memoirs of a Defiant Old Woman

Published by
Garnet Publishing Limited
8 Southern Court
South Street
Reading
RG1 4QS
UK

www.garnetpublishing.co.uk
www.twitter.com/Garnetpub
www.facebook.com/Garnetpub
www.garnetpub.wordpress.com

First Edition

ISBN: 978-1-85964-264-1

British Library Cataloguing-in-Publication Data
A catalogue record for this book is available from the British Library

Typeset by Samantha Barden
Jacket design by Haleh Darabi

Printed and bound in Great Britain by TJ International Ltd, Padstow, Cornwall

To my daughters and my late mother

Weeds Don't Perish – a common German saying

Acknowledgements

I would like to thank Khaled Batrawi, the first person to urge me to write my memoirs,

Diane Langford, a good friend who selflessly spent a great deal of time helping me with editing and encouraged me repeatedly on the many occasions when I was about to give up,

my grandson Nico, who helped with typing and again with the proof reading,

Eve Segal, another friend who did some of the initial editing,

Yardena Cohen, my Dance teacher in Haifa, who introduced me to Middle Eastern rhythms and movements,

Kieran Nugent Sutton, who did a lot of the typing for me with patience and good humour,

Dr. Nadia Taysir Dabbagh, who did so much for me beyond the call of duty while I was in hospital,

and last but not least,

Gaby Forrell, without whose technical skills and unstinting help this book would never have seen the light of day.

Margarete Mundlan — Jutta Ruge

— Margot Flemm

— Elisabeth —

Rehbek Suvarrow

Inge Guttmann

Ingeborg ← Guttmann, my friend

Jutta Ruge, whose fath
a painter; her mother
her to visit me long
it had become unaccep
visit Jews

431

– Traut – Annemarie Bode + Irene _____
+ Rita Bergwerk

April 1937 –
I sit directly
under Hitler

Irene Podiebradt
from Gechoslavakia
father old nobility
mother Jewish,
she returned to
Germany after
divorcing.
A particularly
charming girl

Irene Heilbronn
→ a Jewish friend
with whom I
went to watch
Hitler

↘ Ursula Knüpfer, daughter
of my piano teacher

Part One
1927–1958
Early childhood and emigration to Palestine

Chapter One

It was mid-October when we arrived in Haifa on a beautiful, cloudless and hot day. There was the glittering bay with sparkling white houses, interspersed with dark green cypress trees climbing up to Mount Carmel. The sea was a deep turquoise and it all seemed like a fairy tale scene to me.

I remember little of the actual disembarkation; it seemed at the time that from standing on deck and gazing at the beautiful sight in front of us, we were magically transported to the quayside and were standing amidst a gaggle of relatives, most of them strangers to Mother and me.

"You are lucky, we've just had a really fierce Khamseen for eight days and it only stopped last night."

"A what?"

"Khamseen, you know."

We didn't, of course. Seeing the blank expression on our faces, he continued:

"It's the hot dry desert wind that blows periodically from the Sahara."

The word is Arabic for fifty (*Khamisheem* in Hebrew), as this was the number of days Palestine was afflicted by it annually.

It has long since been translated into the Hebrew as *Sharav* to hide any notion that our languages are so very similar, not to mention that the local populace knew a great deal more about weather and geographical conditions than we did.

Aunts warned my Mother never to buy anything from Arabs and never to employ them.

It was the first time anyone had mentioned Arabs in my presence.

"Who are Arabs?" I ventured childishly.

An uncle pointed out the dockworkers, sturdy men in wide black Salwar pants.

"See those dockworkers? They're Arabs to a man. Dirty lot!"

Given the heat and type of work they were engaged in, it was hard to imagine how else they would look. I didn't recognise racism until years later.

When Mother replied that this was hardly the way to live with them in peace, our new relatives regarded her with a mixture of consternation and pity: she wasn't a proper Zionist at all!

At the time this was certainly true. For Mother, like many other North German Jews, Zionism was something for East European Jews who had trouble making ends meet. I still remember her musing aloud after a visit to Arthur Ruppin, a distant relation from Germany who had become an early Zionist living in Jerusalem and who had achieved considerable fame: "I don't know why he became a Zionist. Such a good family!"

Years later Mother was persuaded to Zionism, albeit a much more benign version advocated by Prof. Martin Buber, who believed in a bi-national state rather than a Jewish one.

He wrote extensively on this vision, but came to be regarded widely as an unrealistic eccentric and the bi-national idea was soon side-lined prior to being forgotten altogether.

In Palestine, the slogan of the time was "Hebrew work for Hebrew workers" – a boycott on any Arab produce or employment. Among other reasons given for the boycott of Arab goods and labour was the one that Arabs were not unionised. However, it was never mentioned that they were not accepted in the Histadruth, the most powerful trade union, expressly formed to cater for the needs and aspirations of Hebrew workers. Yet we claimed to be Socialists. Palestinians in Israel still face shoddy, third-class treatment in most forms of education and employment.

On that calm and sun-drenched day in 1937, though, what I remember best is the beauty of the surroundings, the marvellous clear light and, above all, the cheerfulness and excitement around me: everything and everybody was a great deal noisier than I had ever seen in my ten years! I loved it all and became instantly converted to my new homeland, deciding initially in quite a childish way that I wanted no further truck with Europe. This first instinctive rejection of that continent – admittedly, I knew nothing about any other Mediterranean countries – and my deliberate adoption of all things non-European has stayed with me throughout the years, although I acquired quite a few British and other European friends over time.

Why did we emigrate to Palestine? Certainly not because of Zionist ideals: particularly not on my Mother's part. However, Uncle Julius had two siblings who had become early Zionists, still a rarity at the time amongst West European Jews. His family had come from a far more traditional background in Transylvania. Two of his siblings and their respective families had settled in Palestine around 1925. Their enthusiastic persuasion prevailed, not least after Julius explored the possibilities of finding a livelihood and was guaranteed secure employment with the British Mandatory Authorities as a specialist in electrical engineering. He had been working for Siemens.

We immigrated to Palestine four years after Hitler came to power. There was an increasing exodus from Germany and we followed in 1937. Most of our circle of friends and acquaintances left for other European countries, including Britain, or for the USA. I fear the majority of my relatives were too short sighted to move at all, finding the idea of leaving Germany unimaginable until it was too late. Most of them perished in concentration camps.

The journey to Palestine was a wonderful experience: Omi, my grandmother, as well as Uncle Paul and Auntie Rechi, Mother's sister, came with us on the train to Trieste, where we stayed for two days prior to boarding the *Galilea*, an Italian ship bound for Haifa.

It was twilight when we set sail and there were Uncle, Auntie and Omi, the latter in tears, on the quay. It was the last time I was to see her.

Omi had paid for us to travel first class and our en suite cabin was beautiful. The sea on the first evening was quite rough, although it didn't bother me.

I remember, after dinner, searching the deck to find someone seasick. People who are afflicted in this way tend to lie on deckchairs in the fresh air, so I had been told. The deck was deserted, but eventually I came across a woman lying on a deckchair. She looked pale and wan, although in the dim light it was hard to tell.

"Excuse me," I said politely, "are you seasick?"

"Yes I am," she replied feebly, whereupon I sat next to her and proceeded to question my poor victim about what this disease actually felt like. I didn't get far, however, before Mother got hold of me and dragged me away. To be on the safe side, she dosed both of us with some anti-seasickness tablets Uncle Paul had given her, before we went to bed.

The next day there was urgent knocking on our cabin door. The steward asked loudly whether we were all right. It was 1.30pm. Mother had mistakenly used sleeping tablets, also courtesy of Uncle Paul. But from then onwards the trip was pure pleasure. The sea became calm, the sky cloudless and the four and a half days passed almost too quickly. Early on the fifth morning Mother woke me and we climbed onto the deck, where many others were assembling. We could just see the outline of land ahead, but after a while a mountain seemed to rise out of the sea: Mount Carmel.

Chapter Two

My birth certificate gave my name as Lieselott Johanna Fraenkel, born in the prosperous section of Charlottenburg in Berlin, on 25th May 1927, to Dr. Med. Manfred Fraenkel and his wife, Sella Selma Fraenkel. Lilo, a diminutive version of Lieselott, became my name throughout my early childhood until the great watershed when we emigrated and my much-loved father was ousted by the one man I had always resented.

It was a happy, innocent childhood, in which I was surrounded by the love of Mother, Pappi, grandparents and other adoring relations, not forgetting Deta, my nanny, whose name Marta I couldn't pronounce as a toddler. Deta was a devout Catholic, who sometimes took me and one of her former charges, Peter Rachwalsky, along to church on Sundays, but one day we hurt her feelings when we complained about the stench the man was sprinkling (incense) and she stopped taking us.

I wonder whether Peter was aware that he was Jewish. I certainly wasn't. Christmas with the tree and presents on Christmas Eve, the carols I sang to the accompaniment of Mother's piano playing were lovely, with mounting excitement and expectations until the little bell summoned me to come to the drawing room, where a large beautiful Christmas tree had been erected with presents underneath. So was Christmas day with the great meal, Easter and searching for Easter eggs and last but not least St. Nicolas Eve, 6th December, when I would hang out my stocking the previous evening to find it filled with sweets the next morning. According to tradition, only well-behaved children received these. The ones who didn't make the grade were supposed to find twigs and sticks in their stockings. Speaking to a young German woman some years ago on holiday in Greece, I asserted that surely no child ever received these, but she replied that she did one year.

I was a very agile child and relished almost all forms of gymnastics as well as eurhythmics, something I enjoyed throughout my life and, with the addition of dance and choreography, these have given me much pleasure as well as keeping me nimble far beyond my age. I was so confident in my physical abilities that more than once I made a bit of a fool of myself. During a visit to my grandparents, I was allowed to come along to a eurhythmics class for children aged seven to eight. At the time, I was four years old. Halfway through the lesson, the teacher announced: "Today we are going to try and do a handstand. Is there anyone who can already do it?"

My hand shot up immediately: "I can!"

But, despite trying again and again, I didn't quite manage. Eventually the teacher said, "Well, maybe another time."

"But I could do it when I was young", I insisted and was furious when parents seated round the walls burst out laughing. I was convinced they were laughing because they thought I was lying.

There was a similar occurrence on one of my summer holiday visits to Homburg. The baker's daughter, twenty at the time, had come on her adult size bike to take orders for bread and other pastries. While I was waiting with her by the window in one of the front rooms, I kept looking at her bike.

"Do you like my bike?" she asked.

"Yes, very much."

"Can you ride a bike?" was her next question.

I had never been on a bike, but since I was an ace on the scooter, I was sure there couldn't be that much difference.

"Yes, I can," I told her.

"Would you like to have a go?"

Of course I did. I wheeled the bike to the street and mounted it. I was far too small to sit on it, so I rode it standing upright. The street was on a decline and all went smoothly until I reached the end. Stopping and turning the bike round was a problem, but I managed it by dismounting. I hadn't counted on the incline on the way back: I was swerving madly and two ladies crossing the road told me off angrily. But that was nothing compared to the trouble I got into when Omi, who was visiting, spotted me from a window facing the street.

After a terrible scolding from her, Auntie Rechi and Uncle Paul, the silver lining appeared in the shape of a children's bike. I had to promise to ride it only in their large garden and always managed to fall off it by the gooseberry bushes.

I could also be a bit of a daredevil.

It was a sunny spring Sunday in 1932, shortly after Omi had moved to Berlin. It seemed a pity to stay indoors. Our help had the day off, Pappi had to go out and Mother and Omi were busy in the kitchen.

"I can go by myself." I announced. Mother and Omi were concerned.

In a capital like Berlin crossing a road by myself was a strict no-no.

"But if I just walk round the block I needn't cross any roads."

"Promise you'll only walk round the block."

I promised faithfully. When I already had my coat on, the glimmer of an idea was germinating.

"I'll take my little handbag too."

I knew I had some money in it.

"What for?" asked Mother.

"I just want to look more grown up," I responded. I walked around the block twice to reassure Mother and Omi, who were keeping an eye on me. After that, I continued to walk along our street, Kantstrasse. I knew that if I got as far as Joachimsthalerstrasse and turned left, there was my favourite snack bar.

Once I got to it, I put my coins in the automatic sandwich slot and chose my favourite: an Italian salad and sausage sandwich. With this in my hand, I went to the drinks counter and stood on my tiptoes to reach it.

"One lemonade, please."

The serving attendant frowned: "Who are you with?"

"I'm on my own. Here is the money."

She grumbled about these modern times, but served me. By the time I had finished, I felt that it was rather late and decided to take the tram that had a stop just outside our house. The conductor also frowned.

"Are you going just on your own?" he asked.

"Yes, Here is the fare."

He shook his head in disapproval. When we reached my stop, I looked up and saw Mother and Omi in tears on the balcony. That didn't bode well. I waved gaily to them while crossing the road. It turned out that they had been about to call the police. What was most frightening for them was seeing me cross the road without watching the traffic. It was a long time before I was allowed to go out on my own.

In 1990, after the wall fell, I revisited Berlin with my younger daughter Yael and we retraced the route I had taken all those years ago. I had crossed seven busy streets!

Occasionally we would visit my grandparents in Stettin (now Szczecin). The train journey was always exciting, and at the station at Eberswalde, halfway to Stettin, platform vendors offered 'Eberswalder Spritzkuchen', a local pastry speciality. I always received one. Opa, my grandfather, was a lovely and gentle man, who presented me with a rocking horse for my third birthday despite all the rest of the family insisting that rocking horses were only for boys.

Opa died in 1931, mercifully before the rise of Hitler. He was such a German patriot through and through that the advent of a national socialist anti-Semitic regime coming to power would have broken his heart. Although Opa still celebrated the Passover ceremony, albeit all in German, to the last toast, "next year in Jerusalem", he invariably added devoutly, "God forbid!"

My memory of his death and funeral is very hazy. I was deemed too young to be told about death and on the day of the funeral was sent off with a strange nanny. But I had overheard something about death and a funeral. So when we came across Pappi, who had just arrived in Stettin dressed in top hat and tails, I asked eagerly: "Are you going to the funeral?"

"Yes my darling, I am," said Pappi, "but it's nothing to worry about." Instead of being worried, I was very impressed and boasted to anyone on our way, "my grandpa is dead!"

A year later, Omi, Opa's widow, sold her home in Stettin and moved to a newly built apartment on the top floor of our luxurious block of flats. As I was her only grandchild, she spoiled me endlessly and was always there for me when I wanted to play cards or snakes and ladders. She also always let me win, which was fine to start with, but a little irritating as I grew older.

My first day of school came after the Easter holidays in 1933, at the end of which I, along with all German school children, received a large *Schultuete* (school cone) filled with edible goodies – eat your heart out, Laurie Lee, we did get the present! These cones came in all sizes and I was convinced that mine was the largest. I still have the photo with me in a tartan dress with a white button-on collar, a white beret and a satchel on my back, holding the large cone. There were no uniforms as such, but tartan dresses were a popular school garb.

This was also the day I became aware of being a Jew. Mother had told me the previous evening to say: "Jewish" when asked about my religion, but it meant little to me at the time. For a long time, being Jewish didn't impinge much on my conscious-ness. I continued to go ice-skating with my classmates on an ice-rink not far from us, which served as a tennis ground in the summer. Music blared out from the little hut to which we retreated from time to time to warm ourselves by the enormous stove and sometimes to eat freshly roasted chestnuts.

The usual music was the *Cuckoo Waltz* to which we raced, executed figures of eight and played catch. My first hesitant steps on ice skates had come much earlier, at the age of four or so, on the Lietzensee, a lake not too remote from our area.

Not long after I started school, my right ear came into prominence and has played sometimes a minor and at other times a major role throughout my life. It started with an earache and a fever, which refused to decline despite eardrops and other medications. After an endless week of increasing pain, I ended up in hospital. I remember little about the otitis media operation, but after waking, spent a pleasant fortnight there, where I had a room to myself shared by Pappi, who had his bed opposite mine and slept there every night. The nurses were nuns and the whole experience was enjoyable, without me realising how dangerous otitis media was at that time, resulting in death if not caught before the infection spread to the brain.

By the time I started school I read fluently, despite efforts of family and friends not to teach me, lest I got bored at school. I would go round pestering people, asking them to tell me this or that letter in a book or a newspaper until I had managed to piece it all together. Probably because I was an only child, I read voraciously and remained an avid reader until late middle age, when I started slowing down. These days, it takes me almost a month to complete reading a book, probably thanks to my glaucoma, and I find it hard to imagine that I devoured four or five books a week.

One notable book I read almost through was the *One Thousand and One Nights*. It was part of our extensive library of classics, mainly but by no means exclusively of German literature. My parents innocently assumed that it consisted of tales like the story of Ali Baba, Sinbad the Sailor and so on. I soon discovered that there were tales of a very different sort in it. In fact the bulk of the tales weren't meant for children at all. A great deal of it went over my head. At the age of eight or nine, I didn't fully understand the allegories, but I knew there was something forbidden and arousing that fascinated me.

Many years later I discovered that European parents generally have no problems with what has become *The Arabian Nights* with the naughty bits edited out; Arabic speaking parents generally wouldn't dream of letting their youngsters read the original. I still remember the two – or was it three? – handsome volumes, sumptuous in green leather with gold leaf decorations.

I'm standing in my bed, sleepy and bewildered, with Pappi, my beloved daddy, holding and hugging me. It was summer 1933 and as always, I was spending the long summer holidays with Auntie Rechi, Mother's sister, and her husband, Uncle Paul, in their lovely villa in Southern Germany, Bad Homburg vor der Hoehe, near Frankfurt. It was a pretty spa resort, to which many people came to take the waters from a number of wells with supposedly curative powers. They certainly tasted vile.

"I'm going away for a while," he tells me, "but not to worry, my darling, we'll be together again soon."

A kiss, another hug and he's gone. I'm too sleepy to worry about anything, although I wonder why he woke me up in the first place. Soon I'm fast asleep again. I didn't meet him again for almost 28 years, when I went to visit him in Munich.

Years after he vanished from my life, I found out from Mother that in 1933 the Gestapo had come to arrest him. He had become the physician of the Communist party for totally unfathomable reasons. He had never been a communist or a socialist. He had always been completely apolitical. Pappi had to charm the two Gestapo men with his best cognac, his medals from WWI and his ability to talk himself out of a tight corner. Initially the men phoned headquarters to say there had to be some mistake, but were told that this was indeed the wanted man and that he should be brought in immediately. After some more good cognac and charm, they left in the early morning without him. He took the next fast train going to Switzerland, but broke off his flight in Frankfurt to take a slow suburban train to Homburg to bid me farewell. Pappi died a few months after my visit in 1961 and eventually all the correspondence between him, Mother and myself, along with some photos, were sent to me in Birmingham, where I was then living with my husband and daughters. He had kept every letter and photograph through all the years, a testimony of the unconditional love between him and me.

During my second school year, Renate, one of my classmates, tried to persuade me to join the BDM (Bund Deutscher Maedchen), the girls' equivalent of the Hitler Youth. I explained repeatedly that I couldn't join because I was Jewish, but Renate didn't think this was a problem. Their group leader was so nice, she was sure to accept me. But when Renate told me that anyone who joined the BDM (*eintreten*) could never resign or step outside (*austreten*) I was horrified and found this an insurmountable problem. In German *austreten* is used for resigning from a group or a political party, but it was also the way to ask to be excused to go to the toilet during a lesson.

"Renate, how can you?" I asked her. "I could never manage that!"

I came home quite shocked and told my mother that anyone joining the BDM could never go to the toilet again!

Not long after Pappi left, Uncle Julius came to the forefront of my existence. There were various aunts and uncles visiting us or staying for a while as guests. At that time, any male family friend or relative was termed uncle, the female equivalent being an auntie. Uncle Julius, however, was a permanent fixture. He occupied the room that had been Pappi's study and consulting room. He was the only uncle to correct or criticise me repeatedly and to tell me what to do, so I resented him. Shortly after he moved into our apartment, he set up a desk in my spacious nursery. Although it faced the wall, even his back was an unwelcome and oppressive presence.

Chapter Three

When I was eight years old, there was a repeat otitis media performance, although without Pappi, who was already in Romania. I clearly remember the daily visits of the doctor, an acquaintance of Mother's from Stettin, and his eventual decision that I had to be taken to hospital immediately.

It was on a Sunday and I remember Julius holding me in his trembling arms in the reception area of the hospital. In this hospital, I shared a room with some other children. Initially, I couldn't hear at all after the operation and for some days I didn't quite understand the deeply worried faces of Mother, Julius and Omi as they tried in vain to communicate with me. Eventually, I regained the hearing in my left ear, which became very sharp to compensate for my nearly total deafness in its right counterpart. Thus the lack of hearing in one ear didn't seem to be an obstacle, let alone a disability, for many years. It was during my stay in this hospital that Julius gave me two lovely books of collected cartoons named Father and Son by E.O. Plauen.

They are still with me, almost falling to pieces by now and, with captions translated initially into Hebrew, then into English, have given great pleasure to numerous friends and to my daughters as well as grandsons. They have even come in handy as an aid for teaching ESOL (English for Speakers of Other Languages), which I did for some years after my retirement from full time work. The inscription in the first book, dated November 1935, reads "To dear little Lilo: laugh yourself back to health. Your uncle Julius."

Poor Julius, at least he tried that time.

Very often when I had school friends coming to play, he remained in the room. Nothing was said, but the unease of my friends and of me was palpable. He didn't approve of us climbing onto the shelves, but we compensated once he was gone. After Julius left in 1936, my then closest friend, Inge Guttman, used to come round, often with her slightly older brother and his friend and we would play ships. The shelves, which we could easily reach via the swing, served as gangways, whereas the top of the wardrobe was the captain's deck.

Inge's brother Bubi and his friend were always the captain and his first lieutenant and Inge and I just had to follow their orders, but even so, it was great fun.

My swing, which hung from the door of my nursery, had been a great love of mine from early childhood until quite late in life. It had a seat and a bar as well, from which I could soon hang upside down.

When I did this at college in Dundee, aged thirty-six, the other students became quite anxious: "Be careful, Mrs Braun!"

"Don't worry, I'm fine," and to prove my point I swung backwards and forward still hanging from my knees. I used to swing and still do occasionally, although surreptitiously, in my eighties, whenever an opportunity presents itself.

In the corridor adjacent to my door stood a very tall chest, on its top a large gramophone. I used to swing very high, then on the backward swing haul myself onto the chest and play the old 78 records my parents had acquired: a strange mix of world, light classical and some classical music. Initially, I played them all through out of curiosity, but later I had my favourites, first among them the second movement of Beethoven's fourth piano concerto. It was beautiful, even majestic, but left me wondering what the other movements were like. Why did we have only this part? Mother was uncertain as well. She even seemed unsure how we came into its possession in the first place.

Then there were some folksongs, two of the Volga Boatmen, the second of which has been appropiated by the ABBA group (Now the Carnival is over). I loved them both. Johann Strauss was likewise represented and I found the rhythm of the repetitive Oom-pah-pah quite irritating. Years later, when I listened to the *Symphonie Fantastique* by Berlioz, I found the waltz in the third movement surely the most beautiful one in the world!

Julius, of course, disapproved both of my daring jump onto the chest as well as of overplaying the records, which were still of the winding up variety. Periodically, the gramophone would start winding down, the music dying by sliding lower and slower. You had to hurry to rewind it.

One typical incident with Julius occurred when a classmate came to visit. She was Jutta Ruge, the daughter of a painter, whose Mother continued to bring her even after German Aryans were forbidden to associate with Jews. On this occasion, Jutta and I were drawing pictures. Mine was a house. When I started colouring it, Julius interfered:

"Do you see the windows on the opposite side? They aren't white. From a distance windows always appear dark."

Aged eight, I didn't quite comprehend this, so I chose the next darker colour to white, which I thought was yellow. When Julius saw my yellow windows, he was deeply offended and claimed that I had done this just to spite him and hurt him. I didn't yet realise that he was a master of emotional blackmail.

The incident left me bewildered and resentful. It also made me believe that I was useless at art and I remained mediocre at best until my last school year in Germany in 1937, when our teacher, Herr Terne, drew a beautiful vase full of flowers for us to copy. I liked the vase and the flowers so much that my skills were miraculously restored and the likeness I drew and coloured was remarkably true to the picture on the board. Herr Terne wouldn't believe at first that this was my own handiwork and was only persuaded by all the girls around me who insisted no one had helped me. From that time onwards, my small talent for drawing developed at great speed. I found it irresistible to doodle or draw on every blank bit of paper, much to Julius's annoyance.

Another cause for reproach was my left-handedness. I was made to write with my right hand at school and for a while, as a young woman, was ambidextrous. However, I continued to eat and sew with my left hand and do so until this day, except when eating Indian, African and Middle-Eastern food, when it is obligatory to use the right hand. Equally unacceptable was my left-handedness at sewing, although not at school. There it didn't matter, since the needlework teacher, an early Nazi, put all the Jewish girls in one corner and refused to teach us. But at home, Mother nagged me for ages saying that my efforts at hemming or any other stitches looked awkward. Stubbornly, I persevered, but decided that I was no good at sewing, until years later we were taught some Middle-Eastern, particularly Yemeni, style of embroidery. I was enchanted by it and promptly embroidered the borders of any plain clothes I had in the Yemeni style. That didn't earn my Mother's approval either. She felt it didn't belong on European blouses and dresses.

Chapter Four

Another feature of the time, probably starting around 1934, was our annual attendance at the Temple, as the rather improbable synagogue in Charlottenburg was called. All prayers and sermons were in German. There was mixed seating, an organ and even a mixed choir. After the ceremony of Atonement Day (*Yom Kippur*) flower sellers used to wait as people came out and the men would buy bunches of violets for their womenfolk. The rabbi presiding over all this expressed his opinion, after visiting Palestine in 1935, that although the country was beautiful you couldn't really live there: too many Jews. He eventually made it to Palestine, but was not recognised by the rabbinical authorities there. I doubt he could read any Hebrew. He ended up the as the owner of a bridge club in Tel Aviv.

When I re-visited Berlin in 1990 with Yael, my younger daughter, the Temple still bore the remnants of the original Greco–Roman style with a facade of columns and colonnades in front of it. It has become the Jewish Cultural Centre of Berlin, sadly now guarded by policemen.

At school in Berlin, the real blow for me came when we were separated from the rest of the girls – by our own classmates and former friends. During break one day in 1936, Ingrid Bremer, in whose flat I had previously played and had been most impressed by her room, which was an attic on to which we climbed by a ladder, suddenly decided there were too many of us to participate in the game of catch we were about to play. Ingrid was something of a leader and when she told us to form a line from which she would count out every alternate girl, we did so unsuspectingly. But she didn't count out every second girl: after just a few, it became glaringly obvious she was deselecting the Jewish girls. We were left in a confused and dismayed huddle. Many of our friends were now on the other side, whereas I, for one, didn't like some of the Jewish girls at all.

From then onwards, I became more aware of the increasing restrictions we faced. I could no longer take piano lessons from my teacher, the father of one of my classmates, because he wasn't Jewish. We couldn't go to cinemas, to the beloved ice-rink or even the swimming pool. Eventually, at Easter 1937, Jews were excluded from state schools altogether and I attended a very modern and progressive co-educational Jewish school for one term, until the summer holidays. Mother was quite an exception among our circle of friends and acquaintances: she had decided from the start that a state education would be healthier, a rarity amongst our circle and to my mind revealing some very progressive thinking.

As to the 'creeping' anti-Semitism, there were some exceptions. In the last year, 1936–1937, after Julius had left for Palestine, Mother let Pappi's former study to an opera singer and his wife for some months. He arranged tickets for us to see *Hansel and Gretel*, in which he appeared as the father. It was a great event! I still remember most of the music!

In the summer of 1937 in Bad Homburg, I went off straight to the swimming pool as usual. A sign at the entrance read "Jews unwelcome." I turned away and started walking, but the manager, Herr Link, who had taught me to swim when I was just seven years old and had a warm welcome for me every summer, called after me repeatedly. I pretended not to hear and carried on. I knew he was going to let me in, but somehow wasn't able to accept his generosity. Maybe the reason, albeit unarticulated and not even understood, was that I didn't want generosity or exceptions. I wanted to be able to go because it should have been my right.

There were other Germans who tried to be decent despite the odds. Frau Hagen, who used to clean and do some cooking on a daily basis after non-Jewish employees were not permitted to live on their employer's premises, had to leave us altogether in 1936. I can still see her on the opposite side of the street, red birdcage with Hansi, our canary, in her hand and tears streaming down her face.

And then there were the removal men who came to pack our belongings into two large containers.

This was in early autumn 1937, while I was in Homburg and Mother told me about it later. At lunchtime, the foreman said to her, "we're off for a break now, so, if there is anything you want to add, just do it, we need not know." It was strictly forbidden to take out any money from Germany and Mother was very worried that this might be a trap. However, when the customs officer came for the final inspection, the foreman told him, "It's all right, we've packed everything ourselves."

During our last year in Germany, Mother tried on numerous occasions to explain to me that Julius was my real father and that my name was to be Freund not Fraenkel. I was remarkably obtuse and didn't take any of this in. With hindsight, I had developed a mental block because I could not bring myself to accept that the one man I heartily disliked was supposed to be my real father. One instance stands out in my memory from that period: there was a children's party in the communal park of Bad Homburg in summer 1937. I came first of the girls in a competition for eating whipped-cream-filled meringues with our hands firmly held behind our backs. Both the boy who won and I had to give our names and recite or sing something prior to receiving a prize. When Mother came to visit and I told her proudly about this event she asked,

"And what name did you give?"

Surprised, I answered, "Lieselott Fraenkel, why?"

"Oh, it's just that Fraenkel is such a Jewish name," replied Mother quickly after a short pause.

I was baffled: this from Mother, who had always insisted that I should be proud, not ashamed, of being Jewish? Mother, who had given me a little gold necklace with a Star of David to wear so as to proclaim my Jewish identity? It was only much later that I realised that she had hoped I would have said Freund, the name she had so often tried to explain was my real one. Only on the boat did I finally take it in and for a short while tried to look on the positive side of this event, but after having lived with the Julius who had now become Aba (dad) for just a couple of months, my old dislike returned and indeed deepened.

For the first few weeks we stayed at the place of one of my uncles in Kiryat Hayim, at the time a small settlement in Haifa bay. The freedom and total lack of restrictions were breathtakingly heady. During that time, my mother and Julius were married in a very private ceremony at which I was not

present. Only long after Mother's death did I eventually come to understand her difficult position: for years she had been desperate for a child. Manfred (Pappi), who had spent WWI taking his new mobile X-ray unit to various locations near the front, at a time when the dangers of exposure to radiation were as yet unknown, had become sterile. Eventually, she had an affair with a younger cousin of his, Julius, who had come to Germany from Budapest to study. When she became pregnant she offered Pappi a divorce, if that was what he wanted. His reply was a categorical no and he declared he would recognise the child as his own.

This was exactly what happened. Pappi lavished his love on me. After he had to flee Germany, he no longer had the means to support a family and so Mother eventually married Julius in Palestine. It was not an easy step. I believe the greatest stumbling block was that she was marrying a man nine years her junior, at that time positively shocking.

But I'm almost certain that she was critical of Julius even in Germany. Her economic dependence on Julius made Mother determined that I should have a proper profession so as to be financially independent. She herself would have liked to study further after completing school, but Stettin didn't have a university at the time. At the beginning of the 20th century, in Germany at any rate, young women didn't usually live away from home. And so Mother and her older sister Recha spent their days playing tennis, the piano, and visiting friends and relatives.

I cannot remember what was said at the time, but no doubt Mother explained that henceforth we'd all be known as Freund, all of us one family, with Pappi being excluded.

I didn't go along with this at all, and indeed in my dreams and daydreams I repeatedly saw Pappi, Mother and myself in a house together, with Julius coming to the front door and me slamming the door in his face. These dreams probably started four months or so after he became my official father, but they became stronger and almost violent as my dislike of Julius turned into near hatred.

As to the marriage, Mother told me later that, for a day or two, it was in some doubt as she had no Jewish divorce certificate, only a civil one. This is the case until this day in Israel: only religious and no civil marriages, divorces, birth certificates or burials, exist. Yet Israel deems itself a secular democratic state. It is one of the many contradictions that underpin Zionism.

During the mid to late 1930s, the British authorities were modernising Palestinian telephone exchanges and as a specialist, Julius was sent from one city to another with us in tow. My main recollection of these journeys was feeling terribly sick and Mother rushing me to the nearest toilet at every stop. She had to find the quickest way to these assorted toilets. The reason for my carsickness was that all windows were kept closed, and were often reinforced as a precaution against ambushes and attacks by local Arabs. To make matters worse people smoked inside these airless cars.

What the British mandatory powers as well as the Jewish settlers alike euphemistically termed "disturbances" was in fact a prolonged and bitter revolt, from 1936 to 1939, by the Arab Palestinian peasantry against both the British authorities and the new Zionist settlements that literally mushroomed, often overnight. An old Ottoman law, which still existed in Turkey at the time of writing, allowed a new settlement to remain legally in place once a watchtower and a fence were completed.

This law was frequently exploited by settlers who stole Palestinian Arab lands by night, erected watchtowers and fences, and claimed it as their own. Much of the land had not been fully documented, as villagers knew the boundaries of their respective lands and saw no need to resort to official documentation. Sometimes land was purchased from absentee landlords, many of whom lived in Beirut, which at this time was seen as the Paris of the Middle East.

One of numerous nationalistic songs from that period speaks of the fence and the watchtower, another of "a dunum here and a dunum there" (1 dunum = 1,000 square metres), celebrating as courageous acts of "pioneers" what were, in reality, land-grabs. The late Arthur Koestler wrote a novel on the topic titled, *Thieves in the Night*.

We used to sing these songs enthusiastically without ever realising the glaringly obvious message they contained. Neither did most of us see the contradiction of living in Palestine as Palestinians, yet simultaneously singing about our land of Israel in all eternity. It was Lenin who coined the term "useful idiots" for blindly loyal followers of the Soviet regime. The term could have been specially tailored for us.

Our first location was Tel Aviv, where I started attending the local primary school. On my first day, the head teacher asked my name.

"Lieselott Freund," I stated.

"What's your Jewish name?" He wanted to know.

"I haven't got a Jewish name."

He simply could not believe this.

"You must have a Jewish name!" He insisted.

I felt as if I had been accused of lying, but I persevered. Eventually, after I had rejected his suggestion of Leah, which I disliked intensely, he asked impatiently, "don't you have a middle name?"

"Johanna," I replied, relieved that at last I could manage something positive. Johanna had been my great-grandmother.

"Well, that's Hanna of course."

The trouble with this name was that modern de-Arabised Hebrew doesn't pronounce the soft "H" like its Arabic equivalent, rather it is pronounced Channa, as in the Scottish loch, which I hated. But I recognised that I had exhausted my options and gave in. When I told my parents about it, I was immediately told comfortingly that at home I could still be Lilo as before. But I would have none of it: not only had I undergone two name changes within a short period of time, I was now offered the comfort of having yet another name, albeit my original one. I refused angrily and after a week of not responding to anyone calling me Lilo, my parents gave up. Only in my correspondence with Pappi did I remain Lilo.

Chapter Five

We stayed twice in Jerusalem, on the first occasion in 1937–1938, at the height of the great Arab revolt against the Zionist settlers and the British authorities, and again in autumn–winter of 1939. By that time the revolt had been crushed by the British Mandatory Authorities, although the occasional ambushes and hostilities against the growing Jewish population hadn't ceased altogether. I was unaware at the time of how cruelly it had been crushed: indeed the existence of the Arab population seemed somewhat remote and shadowy, barely intruding upon our consciousness. I can well imagine white children in other colonial countries, India, various African countries, growing up hardly noticing the indigenous population, except as servants, menial labourers or strangers occasionally glimpsed from a coach or car window.

I wasn't too overwhelmed by Tel Aviv, despite living very close to the sea. Mother would often go swimming with me, as our bodies hadn't acclimatised to the climate as yet and felt it was pleasantly warm in December. Occasionally, she would let me go by myself, but she became suspicious when I didn't show any sign of a tan.

"That's because I play with my friends in the shade," was my explanation. It sufficed until the day when, coming ashore from my swim, there was Mother sitting on a deckchair.

"You have been out for forty-five minutes. Most of the time I couldn't even see you!" This put an end to my going swimming by myself until I was almost fourteen.

The only other memorable event from that time was that, after yet another acrimonious argument with Julius, I burst out: "Maybe you aren't my father at all!" He challenged me to go and have a blood test but I prevaricated: I felt that I'd rather not know the truth. All of a sudden Julius threw himself to the floor, hammering on it with his fists and howling like a wounded animal. Mother and I stood by wordlessly. The whole event is still deeply etched in my mind. It was also the only time I saw him so completely out of control.

Jerusalem was very different from Tel Aviv. I loved the city with its granite exteriors appearing rose coloured at dawn and dusk, with its atmosphere of an ancient capital and with the stark mountains surrounding it, carpeted in the rainy season with wild anemones and cyclamen. Much of the area we lived in, Rehavia, was only partly built up, with new and often unfinished buildings only slowly encroaching on fields, rocks and large puddles. What marvellous playgrounds they made and how I loved the wind howling through them! Our semi-nomadic life from 1937, until we finally settled in Haifa in 1941, made it difficult to form lasting friendships, but there were playmates and as ever, there were my beloved books. I continued reading voraciously and almost exclusively in German.

It was in the winter of 1937, at the height of the Arab revolt, that we came face to face with the "Jew-hating and treacherous" Arabs we had heard so much about. On a sunny Sabbath, Julius decided it was a good opportunity to see Jerusalem's old city. As always, he had refused to ask anyone for directions, let alone advice. As we approached the Jaffa Gate, an area completely Arab at the time, a young man appeared and offered to guide us through the old city. A fee was agreed and we all trooped through the gate after him. It was completely enchanting! Today it is difficult to imagine the colourful and noisy crowd in the narrow lanes and steps, with no squares or piazzas that, although more modern and spacious, detract from the character of the place. I strayed into little alleys and byways, attracted like the myriads of flies by the different glittering displays and the multitude of intriguing scents, shouts and chants.

My impressions of historical and religious monuments were rather vague and jumbled on that occasion. In no way could they compare to the souq and its wonders. In a letter to Pappi, I described the wonders of the souq in glowing terms, with drawings to illustrate some of the stalls, the old walls and the wailing wall, at that time no more than a ruin with a modest space in front, quite unlike the very large piazza-like clearing that was later created by demolishing numerous Arab houses and shops.

My parents had meanwhile realised that we were in the midst of a totally Arab area with an Arab guide and became increasingly anxious. I remember various male figures huddling sullenly in doorways or by walls and our guide calling something out to them, to which they grunted brief and dour replies. I also remember my parents repeatedly instructing me to stay close by their side and not to wander off even a few steps, which I found most insulting to the maturity of my ten years.

To add insult to injury, they switched from German to English, which I didn't understand and which I found very silly and annoying. Even today, this belated attempt of theirs to fool the guide into thinking we were British seems quite laughable, considering my parents' dark hair and Teutonic accents, not to mention the fact that the revolt was directed against the British as much as the new Jewish immigrants.

The confrontation came when our guide offered to take us up King David's Tower (unrestored at that time and much smaller). My parents declined, claiming to be too hot and tired, but I declared that I was neither and would go. The guide was keen to take me and promised to take the greatest care of me, as if I were made of glass. He probably felt we were not getting our money's worth, since my parents had hastily foreshortened the tour once they realised where we were. It became impossible to refuse without causing offence and so, promising to be no longer than ten minutes, we climbed up.

It was a little disappointing. The tower was dark and dank inside, with a pervasive pungent, sour smell of donkey urine, the steps crumbling and the guide's explanation of the views not very clear to me. But I had had my way and was returned quite unharmed to my, by then distraught, parents. In no time at all we were back at the Jaffa gate and parted amicably from our friendly guide.

The reaction of neighbours and friends when we related our little adventure was one of total disbelief mingled with horror. Nobody, but NOBODY in their right minds volunteered into most parts of the old city, let alone the Arab part. As for the warnings, admonitions and gruesome descriptions complete with gory details of what might have happened to us, they could easily make quite another story.

These days one can observe the self-same reaction from most young Israelis, who are certain that, were they to venture into any Palestinian city or area without armed military guards, they'd be murdered straight away, despite evidence of Israeli peace activists who enter on a weekly basis.

During that winter, I had yet another ear infection, this time in my left ear, with the potential of making me completely deaf. However, the doctor who came quite late in the evening decided not to take any risks and pierced my eardrum after having given me a short anaesthetic. Despite my ear, I suffered no setbacks in training in arms and using them during the 1948–1949 war; neither was there any problem during my first three years of teaching in Israel.

Chapter Six

In 1939 we went to live in Tel Aviv for the second time. On this occasion, I attended a very progressive school, belonging to one of the Histadruth's, the very influential umbrella trade union's, educational establishments. At the time and well into the 50s, three main types of elementary schools existed in the Jewish Yishuv (settlement): mainstream Zionist, religious Zionist and left Zionist. There were also the British schools, mainly at secondary level, as well as schools of the Alliance Française, frequented mainly by Sephardi (of post 1492 Iberian descent) and Mizrahi ('oriental' i.e. of Middle Eastern descent) children.

Histadruth schools were known to be very progressive. We called our teachers by their first names and there was a general air of informality and friendliness. However, when the school accepted me, it was decided that, since my Hebrew reading and writing were not quite up to scratch yet, I should go to a lower year. This would not have mattered greatly to me: there were quite a few other pupils who were in the same position. But Mother was dismayed about it. The fact that I was almost a year older than the norm preyed on her mind and, as a result, on mine as well. As I became a teenager and even an adult, I tried for many years to hide my real age.

My new school was situated at the Northern edge of the town, amid sand dunes and close to the ruins of a tomb, known to us as the Sheikh's tomb as it was rumoured that an Arab sheikh had been buried there. Our teacher said the idea was very far-fetched and we believed it. Only many years later, after I had begun to understand the deliberate policy of denial regarding any long-standing Arab presence in all of Palestine, I reversed my opinion and now believe that the tomb and possibly a small village or a Bedouin encampment had indeed existed in the place prior to the Zionists' arrival.

I liked the school, made some new friends and developed my first crush, on an unremarkable boy in my class who was good at drawing.

During this period, Mother tried several times to attend Hebrew classes, but couldn't get to grips with it. Probably the reason was that she was always the only one who couldn't even read the Hebrew alphabet. She had no trouble with English and French, albeit with an atrocious accent: her teacher at school had been German and taught other languages as she had believed they ought to be taught.

But this was also the first time I first became aware of Mother's great sense of humour. She had managed to say, "Excuse me, where is such-and-such Street?" Most people, realising from her accent that she wasn't a Hebrew speaker, replied in German or Yiddish – also a problem for us. If they did reply in Hebrew, Mother had to confess that she didn't really understand the language. Walking along the street with her one day, Mother asked a young man her usual Hebrew question about the whereabouts of a street.

"Dear Lady, I am new to this country and cannot understand Hebrew as yet. Do you by any chance speak any German?"

Mother's reply left me gaping.

"Well, if needs be," she said, "I can speak some German too."

She immediately confessed, though, that her situation was identical to his.

Some years later in Haifa, Mother sometimes went with me to an open-air café on Mount Carmel, which was located amidst wonderfully scented pine trees. Mother would have a coffee or a cold drink, while I always opted for ice cream. I remember one occasion when she had coffee and I had my ice cream. When the waiter came with the bill, Mother asked him, "And how much do I get for drinking all the coffee?"

There were many instances like this, although in later years, she neither joked nor sang much, no doubt because of the deterioration in her physical and emotional wellbeing.

In 1940, we moved back to Jerusalem again. The school I attended was more geared to the influx of newcomers who didn't know Hebrew. We were taken out to special Hebrew classes during normal Hebrew lessons.

It was in Jerusalem too, that I attended a proper synagogue for the first – and last – time. In 1939 we rented a flat in a new, U-shaped apartment block at what was then on the border of Rehavia, in West Jerusalem. There were around twelve or more youngsters in the block and we soon formed a gang, with the leader a slightly older girl called Gavriela. We used to play various daring games and on this occasion, as it was Atonement Day (*Yom Kippur*), we were roller-skating along streets that were almost deserted.

"I wonder what they are doing in there," mused someone in the group, pointing to the main synagogue, which was diagonally opposite.

"Praying, of course," replied somebody else.

"Let's go have a look," said Gavriela.

We took our skates off and walked across a rocky field to the synagogue.

The first thing that happened upon entering was that we were separated, with the boys staying downstairs and the girls being sent upstairs. Our roller skates, made entirely of metal at that time, clanged loudly and earned us some disapproving glances from the praying women. We stood in the front row of the women's gallery and became increasingly bored. The officiating rabbi was a small man and almost completely round: a round head, a round face with a round nose, round glasses and a very round belly.

"Just imagine him in swimming trunks," whispered Gavriela.

We started giggling uncontrollably and this, combined with the clanging of the roller skates, earned us an outraged ejection from the synagogue. The boys appeared over an hour later.

"How did you manage to get out? It was terribly boring," they complained.

Chapter Seven

Shortly prior to the outbreak of war in 1939, Uncle Paul and Aunt Rechi arrived in Haifa. They had been visiting Berlin at the time of the Kristallnacht (the night of the breaking glass) in 1938, but took the first fast train back home to Bad Homburg. There they found their house largely undamaged but daubed with anti-Semitic graffiti and swastikas. Uncle Paul flew into a rage and stomped off to the local authorities, banging his fist on the executive's desk and demanding his walls be cleaned up. Amazingly, the executive and his colleagues apologized and promised to send some lads to do the job. They duly came and cleaned up. According to Aunt Rechi, normally particularly cold and undemonstrative, on this occasion she was driven to her knees, trying to hold her husband back from the mad folly of facing down the German authorities. She was convinced she would never see him again.

When not just he, but some youths appeared to clean the walls, they decided to leave as fast as possible. In their case, they had the guarantee of one thousand pounds, a very large sum indeed at the time, required by the British Mandatory Authorities. And so they made it to Palestine just in time.

What's more, they owned half a house in Haifa. Uncle Paul and his wife, being childless, used to travel extensively in the winter months, long before tourism became popular.

In 1926 they had visited Egypt and Palestine, where Uncle Paul befriended a Russian architect, Alexander Wilbuschewich, in Haifa. Wilbuschewich was an early and, according to Aunt Rechi, crazy Zionist, who persuaded Uncle Paul to invest money in the building of a shared house for his family and theirs. When we were leaving Germany, Auntie told us, "If you see some godforsaken dog kennel in the middle of nowhere, half way up Mount Carmel, that's our house."

They were only too happy with the dog kennel, which by then was in a proper street, Pevsner Street, incidentally the street where my school was located at that time. I used to visit them frequently after school. It felt more welcoming than home, with Uncle enthusiastically encouraging me to draw, play on their piano or just chat with him about anything that had aroused my interest from my reading or from school.

Eventually, in 1941, we settled in Haifa in what was to become our permanent home, the first real one in Palestine. Mother took me to the foremost secondary school there, the Reali Gymnasium located not far from the Technion, the Technical University. It was a formal and somewhat forbidding place. Pupils wore uniforms and I thoroughly disliked it. After interviewing me, the headmaster offered me a place at the school. But I implored Mother not to send me there.

We had been told of another, quite new school, named Hugim (circles), which was supposedly very progressive. The name had been adopted from the original circles of Hebrew classes for new immigrants, which the headmaster and his wife had run previously.

"At least let's look at the school," I pestered Mother.

Eventually she agreed although still doubtful, since the school was only going to enter the first candidates for matriculation in a year's time and had as yet no track record. However, as soon as we arrived for an interview, I was certain that this was the right place for me: it was very friendly and informal. The headmaster, after speaking to me, asked one of my future classmates to show me round. She was equally friendly, showed me around and explained that they called their teachers by their first names, didn't stand up when a teacher entered the room and certainly didn't wear uniforms.

Mother gave in and I spent the next five years developing curiosity about history, geography and literature, thanks to some excellent teachers. As there was only one university apart from the Technion at that time, there were numerous academics who were overqualified and who turned their hands to teaching. Our history teacher in particular, Dr Rahel Krulick, always insisted that we think about causes and effects of historic events. We covered a great breadth of history, in complete contrast to my daughters, who both went to school in England and whose knowledge of history was extremely limited and frankly boring: a chronological chain of almost purely British events and endless dates.

Rahel also felt that since we were living in the Middle East, we should learn something of its long and fascinating history, and so we became acquainted with the pre-Islamic era, the rise and spread of Islam and the astonishing cultural and scientific innovations that Europe owed to Eastern Civilisation. In later years, I was told by the headmaster's widow that Rahel had become "very strange" over the years, i.e. she had refused to toe the line and follow the new guidelines of tailoring history to Zionist needs. She took early retirement. Whether she had been forced to do so I don't know.

Chapter Eight

Adolescence is often a time of rebellion and disruptions. In my case, they were extreme. One bone of contention was the at the time purely theoretical idea of my marriage. Like so many mothers at the time, mine would often upbraid me for neglecting household chores, refusing to make myself attractive in her sense of the word, being incredibly untidy (the latter frequently an antidote to Julius' obsessive pedantry) and generally lazy, with the rhetorical query of how I expected to lead a normal, married life if I refused to change. My invariable reply that I had no intentions of marrying were not taken seriously, although I repeatedly and quite cruelly pointed out to Mother that hers were hardly an advertisement for it.

As my hostility to Julius grew, Mother tried to compare him favourably with Manfred in some respects. He was reliable, steady and straight, whereas Manfred had been a spendthrift, an accomplished liar, a skirt-and-trouser chaser and more. Unfortunately, almost simultaneously, at least in my memory, Mother increasingly revealed Julius's defects: selfish, not all that intelligent, petty and small minded. I suppose I was the only person she could confide in.

It is only in retrospect that I began to understand how my mother must have suffered in her second marriage. Even Julius cannot have been happy when I showed my preference for Pappi so blatantly. Mother hid her disappointment and her cooling emotions from him as well as from me. In later years, however, when it became painfully obvious that there was not the slightest chance of me becoming friendlier, let alone loving, towards him, Mother increasingly revealed her own feelings and her own disparagement of him.

When I was fifteen or sixteen, I simply refused to give Julius a birthday present. After much remonstrating and nagging by Mother, I told her:

"All right then, I'll write him a poem."

It was a cruel and harsh poem, in which I called him the great tyrant and enumerated all the endless examples of his selfishness and pettiness. When I showed it to Mother, she looked doubtful:

"Are you really going to give this to him?" she asked.

"Yes," I asserted, although I was not entirely certain myself. It seemed very daring. Mother just shrugged, which in a way took the wind out of my sails. I had expected a fierce argument. Julius read through it and didn't say a word, but his expectation of privilege as the breadwinner didn't change.

I still wonder whether the long years of rationing, first in the war years and then in the years before, during and after 1948, when we received three eggs a week, of which one went to me, two to Julius and none to her (the same went for sugar, flour, meat and a host of other basic foods), did not contribute to Mother's illness and untimely death.

Similarly, the years when on Saturday afternoons we had to go and visit his relatives in Kiryat Hayim, chiefly, it seemed, for him to argue with his siblings. It was a long walk to the bus stop, then a lengthy journey and another long walk in the heat, and the return journey, although no longer in the heat of the day, involved a very long and arduous climb from the bus stop home.

I managed to wriggle out of some of these weekly outings because of various other activities and only joined occasionally, but Mother went as long as she was physically able to and quite a bit longer. He expected it of her. For a long time, I imagined that Hungarian, in which Julius mainly conversed with his siblings and their spouses, was an angry sounding language. Only much later in life did I find out that it isn't the language at all, but rather Julius being angry with them all, since they wouldn't let him tell them how to live their lives.

Chapter Nine

Another illuminating aspect of the war years, discounting a few feeble attacks by the Italian Air Force on the large oil containers in pipelines coming from northern Iraq, was that, for the first time, Palestinian Arabs, or at least some of them, became real to me.

Our new home in Haifa was an apartment on the third floor of a house in Rehov Hashalom/Shari'a As-Salaam or Peace Street. At that time, there seemed nothing ironical in this name. From our balcony, we could see Acca/Acre at the other end of the bay and, on clear days, the mountains of Lebanon covered with a layer of snow all year round. During Ramadan, the old Napoleonic cannons from Acca echoed over the bay in the evening to mark the end of the fast and again just before dawn to signal its start. Although I would hear the deep boom in the evenings, it rarely woke me in the pre-dawn: I slept far too deeply. I used to wonder what it might be like to wake at such an unlikely time and eat a hearty meal. In summertime, A'isha's father and brothers brought their bedding onto the flat roof and slept there, and during Ramadan, they would eat there by the light of a paraffin lamp. It seemed enviably romantic to me to wake to the sound of cannons, to sleep and eat under the stars. It didn't often bother me at the time that no female member of the family ever participated in these events.

A'isha's family were our neighbours and owned one of the four spacious Arab family houses in the street. Peace Street was a steep narrow street climbing up half way to Mount Carmel, not far from the "Persian Garden", as we called the Bahai Garden with its temple. A'isha's family were first-generation town dwellers who had moved to Haifa from At-Tireh, a prosperous village not far away, ironically the location of my first teaching post.

A'isha and I often grinned at each other across the fence while her little brothers and sisters chattered away to me quite unperturbed by my lack of Arabic. Later on, we learned some literary Arabic at school, but it didn't seem to be of much use in conversation. A'isha herself couldn't help me much with grammar, when I got hopelessly muddled with the different noun endings (-an, -en, -on), since her own education had been limited to barely two years. Her older brother, Omar, seemed reluctant to help. He often appeared surly to me, but as the rest of the family were so friendly, excepting the father who was a somewhat forbidding figure in a red fez, I assumed it was Omar's nature. It never occurred to me that he might see me as an intruder.

And then there was Ali, the eldest son, newly graduated from Beirut University, who came to my rescue a few times. I thought Ali was the most handsome and glamorous young man imaginable, and, at thirteen, I lost my heart to him! It was a true schoolgirl crush, my heart beating wildly as I used to walk up the street on my way home, just in case I caught sight of him. If I did, my knees almost gave way beneath me and my face would flush a deep tomato red, including, to my eternal sorrow, the tip of my nose. Ali must have been aware of my puppy love, but he always remained courteous and friendly if somewhat distant. On one occasion, he handed me a fresh tuberose from one of the tubs surrounding

47

their veranda. I pressed it inside a book and kept it for many years.

I believe my initial visits to the house were because of Ali, but later on, when he left to take up a teaching post outside Haifa, my friendship with A'isha and her family continued. I would be in their house at the slightest hint from her or her mother and was content to watch them, or sometimes just the mother, at their household chores which they performed with remarkable calm and serenity while the little ones ran, played and shouted all around us. The Mother never seemed to take a break. Neither did she ever lose her calm and serene appearance.

I mostly remember them sitting cross-legged on the beautifully patterned tiles, preparing vegetables, washing laundry, mending socks or pounding spices. Sometimes the heavy old sewing machine was in use, similar to our own, but whereas A'isha's mother seemed quite relaxed and on friendly terms with it as she ran up simple frocks for female family members and for the little ones, Mother approached hers with a grim face, full of fear and apprehension as if it were some ferocious tiger preparing to pounce. In the drawing room, which housed the sewing machine, there were deep red plush-velvet sofas and chairs, no doubt for visitors, but after a while of shifting uncomfortably on them – they were hot and itchy in summer – I moved to the smooth cool floor alongside the rest of the family. This had the added benefit of disapproval by Julius who often scolded and complained when he found me reading or studying stretched out on the tiles.

Above the sofas, along the walls, hung the round colourfully woven tabaqas (straw mats) that were often laid on the floor for serving fruit. There were delicious juicy figs in the garden as well as some oranges, pomegranates and occasionally sweetmeats and nuts. I still have some tabaqas hanging in my home in London, bought or given as presents on visits to Palestine. In between the mats were framed photographs of stern looking gentlemen. I seem to remember some wearing fezzes and fierce moustaches – presumably various family members and ancestors. On one wall was an embroidered depiction of the Dome of the Rock in Jerusalem. A'isha visited our flat only once and it became quite a formal occasion. I had to promise that Julius would not be present and even so, she came dressed and veiled completely in black and accompanied by Omar, who returned to collect her after an hour. A'isha brought me a hand embroidered handkerchief and we spent most of the time smiling at each other and giggling.

During the war years there was a mutual tolerance in the relations between the Arab and Jewish communities. We had occasional help with heavy laundry from Arab women, mostly from neighbouring villages, and Mother, who showed a healthy disregard for origins or race to anyone she met, knew all about their families, homes and problems with hardly any common language. She also persuaded Julius, who had Arab colleagues, to obtain some samples and recipes of Middle Eastern cooking, which we added to our own repertoire.

A fallah (peasant) from a nearby village came weekly with fresh eggs and I remember him leering at my legs, which in summer were bare, with only mini shorts, the normal gear for youngsters at the time. But it wasn't exactly tactful to show up in them in front of a traditional man. At least I never wore shorts when visiting A'isha.

Haifa in the forties and fifties was beautiful, not nearly as built up as it is now, and with wonderful views of Acca opposite us at the far end of Haifa Bay and beyond, the Lebanese mountains in the distance with a permanent covering of snow on their peaks all year round. In springtime, when Mount Carmel was carpeted with wild cyclamen, we used to race each other to the top, have a rest and later pick armfuls of them to take home. They filled the room with their lovely scent.

We frequently went swimming to Khayat Beach, a lovely long and wide stretch of sand with the sea shelving gently and invitingly. Mostly I went with classmates, occasionally with Mother, but there again she was careful not to offend Julius who couldn't swim and didn't enjoy visits to the beach. What particularly provoked his ire was the sand, traces of which I frequently and carelessly brought into the flat. The Khayat family were wealthy Christians and the beach was open to all and sundry. Its name was changed to the Azure Beach long ago. I sometimes wonder what happened to the Khayats.

Haifa had another beach in a Jewish neighbourhood, Bat Galim, but access to the sea was from rocks with the sea usually quite rough near them. In my early adolescence I became aware of the disdain with which European Jews regarded their Arab or even Mizrahi and Sephardi counterparts and this drove me instinctively to try and look non-European. I exposed myself endlessly to the strong sun and eventually, by the time I was sixteen or thereabouts, I had achieved my goal. To my delight, people frequently refused to believe that I was from Europe, an Ashkenazi, let alone "Yekit", the nickname for Jews of German descent.

Not long before we had also learnt something of the intricate Yemeni embroidery stitches used by many women from that community and I started to embroider various shirts and dresses in the Yemeni style. By the time I was sixteen, I had definite proof. When at some party there was a debate about a German expression, I told the speaker the correct form. He almost sneered at me, "what do you know about German?"

"I was born there," I countered.

"Come on, you're not Ashkenazi!"

Precisely my aim.

Chapter Ten

Mother often remarked on the calm and peace that reigned in the neighbouring household, notwithstanding a lot of noise, shouting, singing, laughing and sometimes crying from the children. There was an absence of bad temper or aggressive behaviour between adults and children and a row between A'isha and her Mother was quite unthinkable. I'm afraid that violent rows between Mother and me were all too frequent during the years of my adolescence and into my early twenties.

Haifa was still reasonably mixed throughout these years and we often visited the largely Arab downtown area close to the port, with its mixture of large and small shops and stalls, a market boasting a wide variety of fresh products, particularly fish, small restaurants and, last but not least, the largest and best stocked bookshop in Haifa, Habash.

One of my classmates took piano lessons from a well-known pacifist Jew, Yossef Abileah, whose music school accommodated Arabs, Jews, Armenians, Greeks and more. Proud parents and friends sat together at the annual concerts.

As a family, we also frequently visited Acca, Nazareth and other well-known Palestinian Arab towns and there seemed to be a feeling of mutual tolerance at the time, although I knew of no other Jewish people in Haifa who regularly visited

Arab homes. No doubt many others did exist, particularly in the mixed areas, and certainly in other towns in Palestine. A Palestinian friend of mine, Leila Mantoura, nee Canaan, who sadly died suddenly some years ago, attended piano lessons given by a Jewish teacher in the completely Jewish area of Rehavia in Jerusalem during these years, while her father, a surgeon, worked in a Jewish hospital.

During all these years, land that was bought, often at exorbitant prices, was then leased to new settlements by the Jewish National Fund. To that end, levies were paid on most goods and all public travel, not to mention the obligatory collection boxes in all shops, classrooms, restaurants, places of public entertainment and in many homes, although not in ours. Money also came from Jewish communities in unoccupied Europe, the USA and various British colonies.

Years later, in 1950 or 1951, I was a delegate at a teachers' union's national conference, during which a discussion took place on whether to continue these collections and levies, particularly in schools. I could not see the point, as by then we had a state and, so I naively believed, all the land we had wanted and more. I was outvoted by a large majority.

Uncle Paul, who would have made a loving father and became someone close to me and was always supportive, was not permitted to practise in Palestine, as he, like many other physicians, was not a graduate of a British university. However, some rather younger physicians undertook their study and examination in Palestine so as to be able to continue working in their profession. Such a one, Dr. Muentz, was the father of one of my classmates, Gideon. Gideon was a particularly pleasant and thoughtful lad. On one occasion, Uncle was outraged when he came across him in the street.

"You are a classmate of my niece, Hanna. What do you think of her?" Uncle asked.

Gideon replied, "For a girl, she isn't bad."

At the time, girls and boys were still enemies and it was only when we were fourteen or so that we had an armistice followed by peace. Gideon's father was a socialist and used to treat poor patients, especially those suffering from tuberculosis, without charge. He became infected himself and died shortly after we completed school. It was Gideon who lent me the book *Native Son* by Richard Wright, which they had at home. For some time after reading it, I decided that if I ever married at all, it would be to a black man. Fortunately, none were available in Haifa at the time. I cannot think of a more disastrous reason for marriage than someone's skin colour or race.

Long since those days, Haifa became upwardly mobile in the literal sense of the word: the middle class has gradually moved to Mount Carmel and even my old school is located there, while our former area of Hadar Hacarmel is now inhabited largely by working-class and poorer citizens.

From the age of fourteen upwards, we used to spend around 5–6 weeks on a kibbutz (an agricultural commune, very poor at that time), during the long summer holidays. As volunteers, we worked in the fields and orchards helping with various tasks. Together with many of my classmates, I embraced the beguiling vision of an idealised future of shared rather than owned property and of building our new land with our hands, if at all possible as pioneer founders of a new kibbutz. One of the tenets of the left-wing section of the Kibbutz movement was that it would only hold as much land as its members could work without hired labour. This ideal is long gone and so are most kibbutzim, in spite (or because of?) the prosperity they gained in the years after WWII, partly by generous reparation money from Germany and partly from the open theft of large chunks of land, not in the least arid, from its original Arab inhabitants.

It was on a kibbutz, though, that I experienced the first puzzling event for me. Two Czech soldiers from the Czechoslovak Free Army had been sent to recuperate in a kibbutz comprised exclusively of Czechoslovak immigrants, all of them completely secular. The two had been bakers in their respective villages and soon volunteered to work in the kibbutz bakery, with the result that the standard of bread, rolls and pastry rocketed to unknown heights.

They took a great liking to kibbutz life and applied to become members. To this day I remember listening to two of the female members discussing the matter while we were working in the orchard. The stumbling block appeared to be that the two were not Jewish. I couldn't understand this at all, why was it a problem in a place where there was no religion whatsoever? Their application was rejected, as was one years later, when an English colleague told me that he too had applied for membership of a kibbutz he had worked on as a volunteer and had been rejected. It took me years to realise that any socialism that is exclusive to one people or group is a contradiction in terms or, worse, a National Socialism, as is the idea of a democracy within a demographic context.

By that time it had become glaringly obvious that the Land of Israel that we had sung about and idealised endlessly was meant exclusively for Jews, although these days this term has become more flexible. In Israel it is actually easy to convert to Judaism so as to counter the "demographic threat". This is becoming more acute, since there is a steady emigration from Israel by disillusioned families, while Palestinians tend to have far more children. Even during my school years, there were quite a few cases of families emigrating from Palestine or waiting for the end of war in order to do so.

Some of our acquaintances from Berlin diliked Palestine for a variety of reasons. German immigrants were usually ridiculed for their traditional good manners and their self-perceived superiority in matters of European culture including literature, classical music, European history and more. To add insult to injury, they had scant knowledge of Yiddish, let alone Hebrew and Jewish/Yiddish culture, and were regarded as inferior.

Many German–Jewish immigrants had married German women, who felt unwelcome and alienated in the increasingly nationalistic country and who wanted to leave as soon as possible, although usually not to Germany. In my class alone, there were five offspring of such mixed marriages. One of them was my classmate and friend, Gideon, although his family was immune to all this and had no wish to emigrate, but three other such families left as soon as they could.

Chapter Eleven

In Palestine we would frequently dance the Romanian *Hora* as well as the *Krakoviak*, its Polish equivalent. This began to change during the late 30s and early 40s. Something new was happening: Hebrew folk dances, nowadays termed Israeli folk-dances, started mushrooming and multiplying. Unlike real folk dances, these were elaborate inventions rather than evolutions. At that time, I loved them unconditionally and was a member of various groups that gave performances.

What these dances really were, and still are, comes down to something phoney, geared to Western tastes with a modicum of Middle Eastern addition: Orientalism in music and dance, much like Rimsky-Korsakoff's "*Sheherazade*" among others. These new dances were a necessary component of the creation of a Hebrew identity: further proof that we really were a people and had our own folk dance traditions.

My eye opener was Yardena Cohen, a gifted dancer and teacher. She was based in Haifa, fairly close to my home and I started attending her classes during my last two years at school and again after my return from my studies and military service in Jerusalem. Yardena was unique in her approach: there were other contemporary dance teachers in Palestine at that time, but none of them were interested in incorporating the dance patterns and rhythms of the indigenous people. Not a few other dancers like me had adopted these totally artificial 'folk dances'. Yardena strove to educate her students in the Middle Eastern tradition. She was quite contemptuous of the mushrooming folk dance movement. Neither did she have much time for ballet, which specialises in elaborate movements alien to the human body and frequently detrimental to it.

And so all our exercises, not to mention improvisations, were aimed at what Yardena termed building bridges between the Jewish settlers and the indigenous Palestinian Arabs.

I loved her classes, particularly Thursdays, when two Arab Jews from downtown Haifa brought along their *oud*, similar to the guitar and its forerunner, and the obligatory *darrabuka* (drum), and we improvised to their very rhythmical beats. It was not too long before I started using choreography based on these rhythms in school for various celebrations.

So as to fit in, I felt the need to adopt a very nationalist stance, probably because even at *Hugim* school, and despite being voted annually without fail onto the class council, I somehow felt I didn't entirely belong. It may have been the fact that I came from a divorced family, a rarity at the time, but mainly I feel that my awful relationship with Julius was to blame.

It wasn't easy to hide, since he continued his moodiness and at home was usually to be found sitting at his desk with his back to the room, not engaging in any conversation. Was it my perception of his presence or did he indeed make my friends feel uncomfortable?

Besides, the fact that in a relatively short period of time my first name as well as my surname had been changed didn't do much for my sense of identity either. Whenever we had to produce birth certificates for external exams, I had to produce three rather than one: my original one, the name change from Fraenkel to Freund and the change from Lieselott to Hanna. I sometimes wonder whether my bi-polar condition, with which I was diagnosed in 2003 aged 76, may have had something to do with all this. Scientifically there's no evidence to support this wishful thinking.

Chapter Twelve

During my school years I became increasingly involved in the Zionist movement as well as the Socialist one, as indeed a large majority of young people were at the time, especially those who stayed on at school after the age of fourteen. We perceived no contradiction: we were combating colonialism in the shape of the British Authorities, and our training, initially in unarmed combat, followed a year later by joining the Haganah (the "defence" underground combatants), seemed an entirely logical step.

The unarmed combat training was great fun. We used to practise in the schoolyard at 7am prior to lessons and the basic idea was to defend ourselves and to attack our opponents with drawn swords, sorry, slip of tongue, sticks.

There were certain prescribed movements, many of them reminiscent of the Gujarati Raas dances, with one vital difference: Whereas the Gujarati dances were joyful, our coach in unarmed combat with sticks would repeatedly shout, "Murder! I want to see murder in your eyes!"

By that time the Haganah – one of whose founders was Moshe Dayan – had been outlawed by the British Authorities. This made it doubly exciting for us youngsters. Initially, Julius objected to me joining since he was employed by the British

Authorities, but one of his brothers came and talked him round. Later I found out that his (Jewish) superior was the Haganah commander of Northern Palestine. I felt really gleeful, but of course couldn't tell Julius or anyone else about it. Instead, I smirked inside myself whenever the supervisor's name was mentioned.

Becoming members of the Haganah involved a secret ceremony at night in a totally deserted spot on Mount Carmel after passing a Bedouin Encampment. There were torches and oaths of allegiance, something akin to what I imagine the Ku Klux Klan ceremonies would have been. Following this, we started training in armed combat as well as in various endurance courses.

Most of our training took place over weekends at nearby kibbutzim, well away from the British army or police. Most kibbutzim had at least some hidden caches. We also went on endurance marches of a week at a time. The one I liked best was a strenuous march from the lower Galilee Mountains to Upper Galilee, lasting one week. Once we arrived, the waterfall of the Hazbani River was fantastic, with a roar so loud we couldn't easily hear each other.

A few of us decided to swim in the river underneath the waterfall, where the waters looked deceptively calm. As soon as we got in, though, we were swept downwards at great speed. There was no question of swimming. We had to cling to each other to make it ashore. Even so, the group carrying our clothes had to walk quite a distance to meet up with us.

I believe that nowadays the Hazbani is one of the most heated bones of contention between Israel and Lebanon and at least two incursions into Lebanon were about control of its waters, which flow from the Mountains of Lebanon into the Sea of Galilee.

As to firearms training, I never became a sniper although I did use a gun in the 1948 war. My speciality was hand grenades, which I never used beyond training.

Chapter Thirteen

After I had taken my 16+ exams, Julius decided that it was about time I left school and started earning. As soon as I announced this at school, a different teacher would approach me during every break to find out why I wanted to leave. It soon became evident that this was not my wish. The head teacher invited Mother to come and speak to him. He offered her a massive reduction in fees. She would only have to pay a third of the normal fee. At that time, no state grammar schools existed, except those of the British Mandatory Authorities, which were regarded as inferior. Julius wasn't best pleased, but could hardly object to such a generous offer.

My interest in arts and humanities made up for my total indifference to maths and science. Our maths teacher, Dr. Nahum Mittelman, was the most gentle and patient man you could imagine. He also loved music. One of my classmates, Sarah, who was a student at Abileah's Conservatory, played the piano very well and so occasionally, especially when exams were approaching or when neither of us had completed an assignment yet again, she would invite Nahum and me to listen to his choices. It was sufficient to keep him sweet.

Matriculation exams were different from the GCSE exams we have in Britain: at sixteen we had to sit just three subjects:

Hebrew, Maths and Old Testament Studies. The latter was obligatory even in completely secular schools. The matriculation exams two years later consisted of at least six exams with one week's preparation time at home between each subject.

At the beginning of the week prior to the official maths exam, I fell ill with German measles and a high temperature. The last thing on my mind was revision of any kind. Although I had regained my health by the day of the exam, I felt completely calm as I entered the large hall of the Technion, where matriculation exams of all Jewish secondary schools were held.

"Well, I'm going to fail this with flying colours, so there's no need for nerves or anxiety," I decided. I thought I would just put my name and details on the paper and then leave the rest blank.

But when I looked at the questions I had a real surprise.

"I think I can do this!" I thought.

"This" referred to a question on stereometry. It was easy to imagine three-dimensional shapes and solve questions relating to them. After this I became confident and even reckless in answering some of the other questions. As we were leaving the hall, I felt that I might just have scraped through. When the results came through, all the papers having been marked by university lecturers, I was gobsmacked. I had received 75%! And this was the one and only time Nahum became angry: "If you can achieve this, what were you doing all these years?"

"I don't really know," I mumbled, "but German measles definitely helped."

Chapter Fourteen

In 1941–1942, the war came uncomfortably close to us. German troops under the command of Field Marshall Rommel were advancing in North Africa and there was great fear that they might conquer Egypt and following that, Palestine. We used to sit with our ears glued to the radio, listening to the news as it came in. Eventually, in 1943, Field Marshal Montgomery overcame the German forces at the battle of El-Alamein in Egypt and Rommel capitulated. What a relief for us all!

The war years touched the Jewish community of Palestine mainly by the terrible common fear, amounting to dread, of practically all European Jews about the fate of family and friends left behind and by the mobilisation of large numbers of young men and women and their recruitment into the British army. Among them were my aunt, Edith, and her husband, Dani, whom I had initially met at the port when we arrived in Palestine. They were childless and thus available for military service. They were part of the Jewish brigade, which was initially stationed in North Africa, but eventually moved with the British army to conquer the South of Italy and thence the rest of Europe.

There was also growing bitterness at the lack of action by the Allied Armies, and Britain in particular, to try and rescue

Jews in any significant numbers or to speak out against the terrible atrocities, news of which increasingly filtered through. Our poet laureate of the time, Hayim Nahman Bialik, wrote a poem of bitter indictment, cursing both the perpetrators of the atrocities and those who stood silently by.

However, in archives made public in recent years it transpired that our first Prime Minister-to-be, David Ben-Gurion, reiterated more than once that had there been a choice between rescuing one million Jewish children by sending them to the UK prior to the outbreak of WWII or only half that number by sending them to Palestine, he would always have opted for the latter. Equally, at a conference in Evian in 1939, there had been various proposals to rescue Jews by taking them to safe countries. This was also scuppered by Ben Gurion, who feared that it would weaken the case for a Jewish state. So much for our humanity.

During my last year at school, a new dispute raged. I wanted to go to university and Uncle Paul had promised more than once that he would help to see me through it.

One day, just a few months before the exams started, I went to see Uncle Paul and Aunt Rechi after school, as I often did. She was out to do some shopping but the door was unlocked. I went in, planning to play and harmonise on their upright piano, which they had brought along from Germany. But Uncle was lying on their sofa and as soon as I came nearer, I realised that he wasn't asleep. He was dead, his mouth half open but not breathing, his eyes half closed but not seeing.

He had suffered two previous heart attacks, but had managed to inject himself in time to save his life. Not this time.

Despite the warm weather, I shivered. I felt completely numb, unable to grasp the devastating reality. Slowly and mechanically, I made my way home, neither seeing nor noticing my surroundings. At home, Mother asked me why I seemed so preoccupied and I made some excuse. I was waiting for the inevitable phone call from Aunt Rechi that was not long in coming. This time Mother questioned me, "But you were there at the time, didn't you notice anything?"

"I thought he was asleep," I mumbled.

Mother shook her head in disbelief, but didn't press me further. She must have seen how shaken I was.

Since there were and still are no civil burials, weddings or other such ceremonies, Uncle had a swift Jewish funeral within twelve hours. What sticks firmly in my mind was that some women from the religious authorities, Hevra Kadisha, came and, according to tradition, were going to make a symbolic tear in my aunt's blouse, instead of the full regalia of sackcloth and ashes.

"Oh no, no!" protested Auntie Rechi, "This is my best blouse, you'll have to wait for me to change into an old one."

Nothing could better epitomise my aunt's nature.

I was sent to stay with Aunt Rechi so she wouldn't be alone. It soon emerged however, that in her usual cold way, she didn't mind in the least being on her own.

But it was certain that financial assistance of any kind had disappeared.

The worst of it as far as mother was concerned was that at the time, youngsters wishing to study at the Hebrew University in Jerusalem or the Technion (the Technical University) in Haifa, both of them the only academic institutions in Palestine, had to do one year's voluntary service. This could be in a kibbutz, within the Haganah, or with the British Police Force in Palestine. The only youngsters exempt from this service were those who went to train as teachers or as nurses.

I was more than ready to do my service in a kibbutz, but Mother foresaw, rightly or wrongly, that I would end up staying, marrying and eventually, if and when I wanted to leave, having no skills whatever. This had been precisely her case with her second marriage and she often replied to my taunts regarding her marriage to Julius that she had had no option: it was either that or ending up in a concentration camp. Mother was also very concerned regarding my age: I had already lost one year and would complete school aged nineteen; to her, starting my training for a profession was a matter of utmost urgency.

I felt that she might have taken the risk of emigrating and fending for herself, but couldn't bring myself to tell her this. After all she belonged to a generation that found such a step, particularly with a child, unimaginable.

Eventually and very reluctantly, I agreed to apply to the Hebrew Teachers' College of Education, also in Jerusalem. It was the most prestigious college in Palestine's Jewish community at the time, but even so, what was I doing training as a teacher when I had no wish to become one? When my teachers at school learned that I was to train at the college, there was much amusement as well as amazement: I had been rebellious, critical and often quite difficult or plain stroppy towards several of them, including the headmaster. They rightly found it hard to imagine that I would choose this profession for myself.

During the long summer holidays that followed our matriculation, three friends and I went to see the Carmelite Monastery from which at that time you had a wonderful view of the coast on three sides, since the coastline round Haifa is almost triangular. We had often visited the gardens of the monastery but this time we ventured inside, following two British soldiers waiting in Palestine to be demobbed. A monk came out and in fluent Hebrew explained that he didn't have any English, only French as the monks were all French. Would one of us please translate into English? All eyes turned to me as I was supposed to be the best at English. Once our containers from Germany had been unpacked, I regained access to all our German books that had made the journey. This led to me becoming a star pupil in English when we started on Shakespeare: we had all his works in German translation at home and I would just pre-read the relevant act or scene.

"I'll translate," I volunteered and a right mess I made of it. The first room we entered had a wealth of treasures and tapestries and our guide explained where they had come from. I translated, and the soldiers said: "These Jews are really wealthy and generous too."

"No, no, there are no Jewish monasteries, these are Catholic," I explained. In the second room the same thing happened. "This is a Catholic Monastery, Jews don't have monasteries," I tried again. But the soldiers persevered in their belief that this place and all its treasures were Jewish. After the third room I gave up and left them to their delusions.

When we were about to leave, our guide beckoned to me to stay behind.

He disappeared briefly and returned with a copy of the New Testament in Hebrew, which he gave me as a sign of appreciation.

I felt embarrassed and guilty: I hadn't even managed to convey to the soldiers that the monastery wasn't Jewish. It took a long time for me to realise that I should have said Christian instead of Catholic.

As to the New Testament, it struck me as rather bland after the bloodthirsty descriptions and sexual innuendoes of the Old. In fact, I never completed reading it.

In due course, an invitation for an interview at the college arrived. I simply sat on it, hoping that if I forgot to reply I wouldn't be accepted. However, a former school friend unwittingly revealed it to Mother.

She questioned me in my mother's hearing about not having heard as yet from college. According to her, everyone had by now received either an invitation or a rejection. Once she left, Mother wormed the truth out of me and made me reply there and then. In due course, I was interviewed, accepted and at the beginning of term in September 1946 moved to the suburb of Beit Hakerem, a lovely, pine-scented suburb of Jerusalem where the college was situated and where most of the houses had small basement flats or rooms to let to students during term time, while in the summer months it was popular with guests coming for the fresh air and the calm.

Chapter Fifteen

I found lodgings in a house that had two basement studio flats, occupied by the only daughter, also a student at the college, and a couple of other students. Upstairs was another spare room, which I shared with a younger girl, who became my room-mate. One of the basement rooms also had a piano, and on one occasion not long after settling into my lodgings, I heard someone play Mussorgsky's "The Old Castle" from *Pictures at an Exhibition*. It was so beautifully played that I rushed down to see the player. It was a young music student, Meir, and I fell in love with him instantaneously. Unfortunately he was also a great womaniser.

The college brought me little joy and my absenteeism became so bad that, after the first term, a letter was sent home with a warning that, unless my attendance improved, I would be excluded at the end of the first year.

Mother was horrified.

"How can you excuse such sloth?"

"You wanted me to go to college. I never did!"

"You would never persevere in any kind of freelance job, you're just too lazy. So what will become of you? "

It had been my ideal to become a journalist, dancer or artist.

To Mother the mere thought was terrifying. She firmly believed that the only job I'd be able to hold down had to be in regular employment. She was also wary of anything that suggested a Bohemian lifestyle.

Whose judgement was saner, given all the circumstances? After endless scenes and rows, I eventually gave in and promised to attend college more regularly. But my attendance only improved marginally thereafter. My heart was not in it at all. The only subjects I really enjoyed were physical education, which involved a great deal of gymnastics as well as eurhythmics, similar to the aerobics classes we have today, and philosophy, or rather an introduction to it: the tutor for this subject, a professor from the university, was outstanding.

As early as 1946, Jewish terrorists (from the group that was later to produce PM Begin) had planted a bomb in Jerusalem's King David Hotel, which was occupied by many British officers. It was unacceptable carnage, with many dead. A lengthy curfew was imposed immediately and tensions escalated from then on.

At the start of the second year of college, tensions continued to mount, with terrorist attacks by Etzel (ex-Beitar) and Stern gangs who murdered British soldiers and officers, with frequent curfews imposed by the British, with desperate attempts to land illegal ships packed with survivors from Europe and with increasing demands for a Jewish state. Only recently has it come to light that Ben Gurion was himself involved in preventing the hapless refugees on the *Exodus* boat from landing anywhere but in Germany, whence they had fled. Both France and Denmark had offered to let them land on their shores after the British prevented them landing in Palestine, but for our first prime minister-to-be, the refugees' importance was solely their use as propaganda material.

The 1947 declaration by the United Nations of the partition of Palestine and of the creation of a Jewish state was greeted with wild jubilation and all-night street celebrations. We were somewhat taken aback by the grim and worried faces of Arabs the following morning: little did we realise that fighting had begun and that expulsions were already occurring in other parts of the country.

Tensions continued to mount between the Mandatory Authorities and Jewish terrorists, with the latter kidnapping and murdering British soldiers and policemen. As a result, there were frequent curfews as well as arrests. Hostilities had also broken out, with Haganah attacks on some Palestinian villages, but neither my friends nor I were aware of this because of the siege on Jerusalem.

The British were getting jittery, sometimes in a somewhat silly way. I was with a group of students sitting in our pine scented garden one night, drinking Arabic coffee, singing and harmonising, when a group of armed red-berets, the shock troops at the time, surrounded us, guns pointed and demanded our ID cards. Mine was just upstairs, but others had to return to their lodgings with armed escorts, to present theirs.

Since January that year, most young students and other young people had spent alternate nights on guard duties for the Haganah in the hills surrounding Jerusalem. In the cold Jerusalem winter, the gun often felt as if your hands were frozen to it, not to mention the painful chilblains I acquired on my feet. During this winter I was asked to take a pistol from one (illegal) Haganah office to one of their outposts. The pistol was well hidden inside my jacket, or so I thought.

But I soon became aware of two British soldiers following me and talking.

"She's got a kilt! She's wearing a kilt!" they were saying. They sounded quite excited and my heart did a somersault. I had never heard of a pistol called Kilt. I hurriedly entered the nearest tallish apartment block and raced to the fifth floor. "*If they follow me, I'll ring the bell and ask the tenants to hide me*", I decided. Nobody followed. After some ten minutes, with my heart still drumming, I went downstairs and cautiously peeped out in all directions. Nobody. I got to the outpost without any further scares.

A few days later I met a friend whose English was better than mine.

"Deena," I asked her, "Do you know what a kilt is?"

"It's a Scottish skirt, why?"

"I just wondered, because some British soldiers were following me and kept saying I was wearing one of those".

I left out my panic. It would have felt too stupid.

In early summer 1948, we finished our studies. Jerusalem had been under siege since winter and there was no electricity, little petrol or other fuel and very little food or water.

Many of us, however, had by then experienced the first of many deeply disturbing shocks: the massacre at Deir Yassin. Early one morning in April 1948, a friend burst into my room with tears streaming down her face.

"They are butchering everyone in Deir Yassin!" she cried.

It took some time to sink in: Deir Yassin was a peaceful small village on a hill to the right of our outpost and close to the suburb in which we had our lodgings. Some of their fellaheen (farmers) would come regularly to sell us their deliciously fresh produce. Even during the 1936–1939 uprising Deir Yassin had not become involved in violence.

The senseless brutality of such slaughter was incomprehensible. Even more despicable was the parading of some of the male villagers in an open van through the streets of Jerusalem prior to their being shot.

Our only comfort, if such it could be called, was that the atrocity was perpetrated by the Stern gang, forerunners of Likud.

That fig leaf was torn from us when, a few months later, Stern and Etzel members were incorporated into the regular army and their commanders became our officers. Complaints fell on deaf ears. We now had one state with one army, we were told. At this perilous time, everyone was needed in the defence of the fledgling state and meting out punishment would be counterproductive.

Nowadays it is of course widely known that Deir Yassin happened with the full knowledge and tacit cooperation of Ben Gurion, although the main protagonist had been Menahem Begin, leader of the extremist right-wing Beitar movement, which later merged with other extremist/terrorist parties to form the Likud party. Begin himself, after spending many years as leader of the main right-wing opposition party of the Israeli Parliament (Knesset), was elected Prime Minister in 1977. By that time Israeli society had shifted to an ever more extreme and increasingly violent stance, so that such a move became generally acceptable.

However, even now too many Israelis and/or Jews prefer to bury their heads in the sand, rather than read the available documents, archives or books written by their compatriots or co-religionists.

In fact, although unknown to us in Jerusalem, expulsions and ethnic cleansing had started earlier. In a way Begin regarded Deir Yassin as a test case. In his memoirs he wrote: "After Deir Yassin we moved through the land like a knife through butter." According to leaders of the Palmach (shock troops of the Haganah), they too regarded Deir Yassin as a test case for the Stern and Etzel gangs, newer versions of Beitar. These leaders wanted to see whether the terrorist groups were capable of conquering and holding a place rather than just committing spurious acts of violence.

During that summer, there was a brief truce and I went home to Haifa for a week. The normal Jerusalem–Tel Aviv route was still too hazardous because of frequent ambushes and attacks from the surrounding hills, especially from Latroun, a Palestinian fortress for which the Haganah and later the Israeli Defence Force fought many battles without success. It remained in Jordanian hands till the Six Day War in 1967.

Volunteers, mainly from the Haganah, had meanwhile constructed a fairly rough road winding down the back of the Jerusalem–Latroun road. It was named "Burma Road" after an occurrence during WWII.

The original Burma Road hadn't been a road at all, but a hurried retreat through the Burmese jungle. It had been an unimaginable feat led by Sitwell, a graduate of West Point Academy. When all other officers were airlifted from the jungle because of the Japanese army getting very close, Sitwell announced that he preferred to walk. He led a motley group of British, Chinese and Burmese soldiers successfully through the Burma jungle to escape the Japanese army that was hot on their heels, and despite the odds they made it to India.

Our Burma Road was a rough road and consisted mainly of lorries carrying wounded soldiers who couldn't be operated on in Jerusalem, which had no electricity, hardly any water and other essentials. The journey to Tel Aviv took seven hours rather than the normal one and a half. Those of us who were not wounded alternated between walking and sitting in one of the vehicles. It was much more pleasant and less stifling.

When we finally reached Tel Aviv, we were quartered in what used to be a guesthouse. In Jerusalem no one had heard of Dior's "New Look", which expressed the general mood of most women: after years of rationing and making do, they were delighted with longer and voluminous skirts.

"They are lovely," I told friends, "but they make me feel almost naked."

Many agreed. But we were at last kitted out with uniforms. Although these were only knee length, I felt superior to modish civilians.

When I finally reached home, I was in for a shock: During my absence, the "liberation" of Haifa and of many other towns and villages had occurred: Jaffa, Afula, Safad, Lydda and many more. We had been unaware of any of this in Jerusalem, being cut off by the siege.

The inhabitants had been driven out, sometimes by straightforward attacks, at other times by different means, often by deliberately terrorising people. In Haifa, for example, Palestinian Arabs in mixed areas had been given 24 hours to leave; armed soldiers ensured they complied. The predominantly Arab downtown business area was cleared as well as purely residential areas: our neighbours as well as the owners of the three other Arab houses in the street shared this fate. My Mother recounted the story with tears.

"This is wrong. One day we'll be held to account for this."

Julius, on the other hand was beaming with pride. He had been one of the volunteers from Haifa who, although too old to bear arms, were taken in lorries to the main road, out of Safad in the Galilee, and given sticks with which to beat the fleeing Palestinian Arabs, should they offer any resistance to their expulsion or try to flee to the surrounding hills. The volunteers were placed on both sides of the main road.

The term "ethnic cleansing" was as yet unknown; it certainly was a very apt description of what was, and indeed still is, happening.

The large shops and business premises downtown were now "liberated" and in Israeli hands. Only one Arab quarter remained for many years, Wadi Nisnas, a small, largely poor, ghetto-like part of Haifa. What had become of our Arab neighbours, indeed of all Haifa's large Arab population, many of whose families had been settled in that city for hundreds of years? It was a nagging doubt that refused to go away.

The differences in my parents' attitudes showed most strongly when, not long after WWII, former German citizens were permitted to claim compensation for lost/murdered relatives as well as lost employment and possessions. Julius received a generous sum from Siemens and pressured Mother to apply for both my grandmother and for Pappi and his X-Ray Institute.

"You cannot compensate for the dead with money," Mother persisted. After much pressurising and after quite some time, she agreed to apply for compensation for the X-Ray Institute, which is how we found out Pappi was still alive. He was making the same claim.

Whereas German Jews found it easy to receive compensation directly from Germany, most survivors from Eastern Europe were told that their claims would be handled by the Jewish Agency in Palestine and thus lived for the rest of their lives in abject poverty, while their compensation money was used to grab or sometimes buy more land (from absentee landlords) and to build up a formidable weapons arsenal, which later included nuclear stockpiles as well. Prof. Norman Finkelstein, himself a son of survivors, researched this scandal and wrote about it extensively in *The Holocaust Industry*. As a result, he lost his tenure in practically all American universities.

Hostilities escalated sharply after the unceremonious departure of the British in May 1948. Having for years played the game of divide and rule, successfully contributing to the animosity between the Muslim and Christian Arabs and the Jewish communities, they washed their hands of the affair and left the sides to their own devices. However, most British police stations, in the main well-fortified and stocked with ammunitions, fell into Jewish hands, as did prisons, radar stations and warehouses. Pure coincidence? I now wonder.

Following my return from Haifa in the summer of 1948, I was assigned to a regiment commanded by Moshe Dayan (later General Dayan, Chief of Staff, later still, Defence Minister). By that time, the Haganah had morphed into the fledgling Israeli Defence Force. We were stationed at the former British Police Station in Abu Ghosh and I found a small room halfway between the ground floor and the second floor, with a separate entrance.

"I'm coming to your room tonight," announced Dayan without any preambles.

"No, you're not!"

Next morning, I was ordered to move to the dormitory downstairs. Someone more pliable or obedient inherited my room. It was one of many reasons that made me despise Dayan.

He had "liberated" numerous towns and villages and used to boast freely of his fear-striking tactics. He had ordered his troops to release a veritable deluge of shrieking sirens, careering searchlights, massive explosions of shells, grenades and other ammunition, prior to mounting an attack on these places. By that time, most of the inhabitants had fled in sheer terror. Dayan was rather proud of his successes gained by this method. I believe he used it often. The fact that the inhabitants, like all Palestinians who had fled or who had simply been away from home during the "Independence War", had lost any right ever to return was left unmentioned.

Indeed, for a long time, far too long I realise with hindsight, it was so much easier to believe the propaganda we were bombarded with: the bulk of the Arab population had fled despite Israel's efforts to reassure them and to persuade them to stay put. Moreover, Jews from a variety of Middle Eastern countries were suffering persecution and peril and had to emigrate, or so we had been led to believe, so it was a fair exchange. It was not until the early nineteen fifties, when I encountered some of these "persecuted" immigrants, that a very different picture began to emerge.

Chapter Sixteen

In early 1950, all female teachers and nurses were released from the army and I found it easy to obtain my own release. But I still neither wanted to teach nor to come home. I found accommodation and subsisted as an au pair, while still trying to regularise my relationship with Meir, the young music student whom I had met and fallen in love with during my first term at college.

My delaying tactics and infrequent letters worried Mother to the extent that she appeared out of the blue one day. She persuaded me to regularise my position with the army and to come home and find a teaching job. Shortly after that, I started my first teaching post in At-Tireh, formerly a prosperous Palestinian village, which we had often glimpsed from the main Haifa – Tel Aviv road and the village from which A'isha's family had originated. I was astonished to see the fine, modern school building erected and then abandoned by the villagers: the general perception by the majority of Israeli Jews was that Arab village dwellers, with very few exceptions, were illiterate.

The village was now inhabited by new immigrants, the bulk of them from Bulgaria and Turkey. Initially, we had no means of communication, but in time it became clear that many of our pupils' parents were less than happy in their new homes.

All the Bulgarians had come from Sofia and were used to big-city life. The Turks also felt that the wonderful promises of life in the Jewish homeland had failed to materialise. All of them felt unneeded and even unwelcome. They had been dumped in abandoned villages if they were lucky and were usually unemployed or overqualified for the jobs they were doing. The young men, of course, had immediately been drafted into the army.

But my initial reluctance regarding my job did not abate. I disliked teaching and felt dissatisfied. My absences were frequent and the only part I enjoyed was choreographing various dance and dance drama activities. It was to be many years before I came to like and eventually to enjoy teaching.

My opportunity to meet some of the young soldiers who were drafted into the army almost as soon as they arrived, came when I was called up to go on reservist duty. In February 1952, half way through the school term, I was sent to Eilat for a month. At that time, it was nothing but a military camp on the shores of the Red Sea.

When I arrived, I was told: "You are a teacher of Hebrew, so you can teach some of our new immigrants."

The hostility of the twenty-five or so young men I encountered the next morning shocked me: they wanted to learn no Hebrew! One young Yemeni who spoke Hebrew explained that all of these men from various Asian countries, Morocco and the Levant had left settled and contented lives in their former homes. They had been persuaded by the constant urgings of Zionist propaganda to come to the aid of the new Israeli state, which was in danger of being destroyed by the surrounding Arab states, as indeed were their own communities. They had been made to feel needed, perhaps essential. What they had not been told was that their main role was to act as cannon and demographic fodder, to decrease the gap between the majority of Palestinians and the Jewish community. On arrival, they were sprayed with DDT at the port of entry and then crammed into extremely primitive reception camps. Within a week or two, they were drafted for a three-year term into the army, often ignorant of the whereabouts of their families and how they were surviving.

They were well aware of the different treatment accorded to European immigrants, whose camps were far superior, who received help in finding suitable accommodation and who were quickly given jobs. Vast numbers of Eastern immigrants now wished to return to their countries of origin as soon as possible; the Indians even held a sit-down strike in central Tel Aviv demanding their fares back. Very few had this wish granted.

One difficulty was the very high level of taxes levied at the time on Israelis travelling abroad.

This was compounded by the fact that, at that time, all Jewish immigrants, on arrival in Israel, had been automatically made Israeli citizens without being informed properly, let alone consulted or asked for consent. As a result, many had lost their original citizenship.

On a recent visit to Palestine and Israel I met an Iraqi who had been part of this influx. He told me that he still felt bitter about what had happened to him, to his community and to all the other non-European immigrants.

As to A'isha's family home, strangers now lived in the house and I refused even to look in their direction. After a long time, when I had been teaching and living in Haifa for around two years, I was returning home late one evening, with the ever faithful Buti (real name Aharon), the most serious of my various suitors, who genuinely loved me and was keen on marrying me, in tow. It appeared there was a party in full swing next door: a long table had been set out on the large front patio with many people seated around it, eating, drinking and chatting. At one end of the table a group of musicians were playing on the traditional oud, darrabuka and ney (Middle Eastern type of violin) in the Middle Eastern rhythms that I had grown to love.

There was a singer who appeared to know many of the guests. He sang a verse addressed to one or the other of them, which was greeted by laughter from all. After this, the guest at whom the verse had been directed stood up and replied to the lyrics, followed by more laughter. It was a little similar to the Trinidadian calypso, but at the time I'd never heard anything like it. I was rooted to the spot despite Buti's urgings, with the new neighbours calling out repeatedly to invite us over. The atmosphere and the music melted my hostility to the usurpers and eventually we joined the party. We were shown great hospitality with people pressing very tasty food on us, while the house owner explained that they were all from the Baghdadi Jewish community. It turned out to be an engagement party and, so the owner proudly told us, the musicians had come from Jerusalem and were considered the best in Israel.

Chapter Seventeen

After two years in At-Tirah, I managed to move to a post in Haifa that involved far less travel. I also continued to develop my choreographic skills, much to Mother's disapproval. She saw little sense in an extra-curricular activity that was time consuming, unpaid and according to her quite a thankless job. She was wrong regarding the third assumption, however: there was a great deal of appreciation from pupils, colleagues and parents. Most important to me though was that I loved doing it and have continued my involvement with dance, dance-drama and choreography almost constantly throughout my life.

During my teaching years in Haifa, pressure increased on me to get married, not just from my mother, but from various neighbours as well, according to her. People wanted to know why I didn't get married to the young man who was my faithful companion but quite an unsuccessful suitor during all this time, until I faced him with my decision to marry someone else. Buti was an intelligent, kind and thoughtful person with a great sense of humour. The only, and for me, insurmountable problem was that I found him physically totally unattractive. I tried to explain to Mother that I would never be able to stay faithful to him, but met with little understanding.

✧

In late 1951 I first encountered Ernest (originally Arnost in Czech, to his Mother always Ernsterl, in Palestine, Amos, and finally, in Britain, Ernest), my future husband, when I went with friends from our folk-dance group to eat at a Middle Eastern restaurant in downtown Haifa after a practice session. He was sitting in the same restaurant with a friend, another of my would-be suitors, and we all joined together.

On this occasion Ernest, who had recently returned from completing his university studies in Prague, struck me as rather distant, superior and not particularly pleasant.

One day, a few months later, I went with a friend of mine to listen to a new recording of classical music the friend had on an LP, a new invention, and met Ernest again. I had not yet learned to trust my first instinctive impressions and so, encountering him a second time at the mutual friend's apartment, I became quite attracted to him and thought him handsome as well as pleasant.

I wonder to what extent the pressure to marry had played a role. He seemed by far the most feasible and attractive choice, although I was aware that I hadn't fallen in love. And although my mother had been so desperate to see me married, she had grave doubts about him, as did her closest friend in Haifa. Both were concerned about the unhealthy Oedipus-like love between him and his "mummy". But I had made up my mind and wilfully blinded myself to possible problems of incompatibility, particularly as to our very different temperaments.

Ernest told me after I first met his beloved Mother, who at the time of our getting together had been visiting her eldest daughter and family in England, that had she not approved of me, he wouldn't have continued seeing me. I brushed even this forewarning aside. The only man I'd have considered marrying before I met Ernest would have been Meir.

Yet in my innermost being I knew well that I should never have rejected Avraham, a co-student at the Hebrew College of Education in Jerusalem. Avraham was one of a group of students who had served with the British Army during WWII and upon release received a grant to study. Thus they were somewhat more mature and spoke fluent English. He was an intelligent, somewhat serious young man whose interest in me, although he made no declaration at any time, was quite obvious. He was also very tactful and sensitive and when he found me unresponsive made no further advances. Although I wasn't particularly attracted to him, I admired his steady, reliable temperament. Moreover, I found his decision to teach in Palestinian schools, to all of our great surprise, both courageous and admirable. I believe that there are, or certainly were, many young women who did not end up with their first choice for a variety of reasons, in my case a trivial one, despite my still hankering after Meir.

Finally, on the evening when Ernest's parents came all the way to mine, expecting us to come out to the balcony where the four of them were sitting, to announce our intention to marry, Ernest got cold feet. He wondered whether it would not be wiser to delay such a weighty announcement. This was too embarrassing.

"Agreed," I replied, "but in this case, I don't believe we should meet any longer." He came round, but ever after teased me that he hadn't married me, rather, I had married him. How serious was he? Was he aware that he was undermining my self-esteem very badly? Looking back on all these unhappy years now, I feel I did the wrong thing to marry him but the right thing to divorce him.

✧

We were married at a very modest but pleasant ceremony on 1st October 1952. As there was, and indeed still is, no civil marriage or for that matter burial in Israel, we had to put up with a slightly farcical religious ritual on Aunt Rechi's veranda and in her living room. On photos from that day, I can see plainly how ill Mother looked. She had been unwell for over two years. During that time and before I met Ernest, she was in hospital for a few days for a bone marrow extraction and examination and it appeared that she was suffering from a particularly malign strain of leukaemia.

Not long before my marriage, Mother kept pressing household items such as our sewing machine, beautiful cut glass vases and other porcelain items on me. To my remonstrations of not needing any of these things in the foreseeable future, her reply always was: "He isn't going to give you anything".

Mother was very clear-headed about the seriousness of her illness. She knew she was dying long before any of us suspected it.

She had developed an abdominal growth and her doctor wanted her to undergo an exploratory operation to determine whether the growth was malignant. By that time, I'd just discovered that I had unintentionally become pregnant, all of nine days after our wedding, although we had been sleeping together for months beforehand. Mother refused the operation and gave as the reason that she wished to become a grandmother first, much to the consternation of her doctor.

Many years later, when I met Manfred again in Munich, he told me that on one occasion during that period she had hastily copied the results of her first preliminary examination while her doctor was out of the room and posted them to him. He replied in a very neutral and indeterminate way, he told me, but he knew immediately that her situation was hopeless.

Chapter Eighteen

Ernest had obtained a post as assistant lecturer in physics at the Hebrew University and not long after we married we moved to Jerusalem once again. I had always loved the city, although a great deal of its fascination, much of it in the old city or East Jerusalem, was no longer open to us: it now belonged to Jordan. Initially we stayed in a very modest pension, in which we shared a kitchen and bathroom. Once my pregnancy had become established beyond doubt, we rented a flat in a house in Baqa'a, formerly an entirely Arab suburb from which the inhabitants had fled or were expelled. (On my penultimate visit to Palestine/Israel, I learned that it has now become a very desirable part of Jerusalem, developed and owned mainly by wealthy American Jews.)

The house in Reuben Street had been a handsome and well-built one, but was now divided into five smallish apartments. Our neighbours were a mixed lot. Upstairs diagonally, in one part, lived a family of Arab Jews from the old city with endless numbers of girls (well, only six really) and then at last a boy who was spoilt by all the females of the family. He was so spoilt that other children in the street often refused to play with him, with the result that his Mother would descend into the street shouting and screaming in his defence. She even threatened violence and the other kids were very scared of her. Eventually another boy was born, but we left for good when he was still a baby.

In the basement flat underneath ours lived a widow with her little boy. She was equally a great screamer, chasing her little boy, who frequently didn't want to eat all that his Mother put before him, with screams of "I'll kill you!"

She looked down on the family in the apartment above ours and used to tell me that they were not like us, by which she indicated that they were Asians. They were originally from the old city's Sephardi community, particularly courteous, gentle and friendly. After they moved out, a family of new immigrants from Morocco followed. On one occasion we were invited to a wedding meal but it was disappointing: the food wasn't Moroccan at all, but a poor version of European cooking. Lastly, a family of new immigrants from Poland occupied the front part of the house that was adjacent to our back part. I knew them less, probably because we didn't share a common yard and entrance.

On one occasion, shortly after Yael was born in 1957, during a particularly severe winter, this neighbour came round to tell me that although she had spent most of WWII in Siberia, she had never felt as cold as this! I imagine that in Siberia there was more protection against the cold, something our houses sadly lacked. The houses were wonderfully cool even in the worst Khamseen, but woefully inadequate when temperatures dropped to below freezing in winter, despite snow falling practically annually in Jerusalem and the surrounding mountainsides.

These days modern buildings take the cold winters into account and central heating is more widespread, although not in Palestinian villages, whose inhabitants are far too poor to dream of such luxury. I found their level of cleanliness amazing under such circumstances. Even with only cold water that has to be heated for washing and showering, people keep clean.

Opposite our house stood a handsome building owned by an Arab widow, a Christian from Acca. She had moved to Jerusalem with her three children but never spoke about her reason for moving. She lived on the ground floor of the house and had let the other floors to Jewish families.

I took to visiting her occasionally since nobody else spoke to her and her children. Among other things, she revealed that her eldest son was studying in Beirut, but communication was difficult. All letters had to go via the Red Cross.

At the time, Ernest and I had already become aware and very critical of the treatment of the remaining Arabs in what was now Israel. This was explained away by "security" needs: dangers had to be faced up to, especially those posed by the *fedayeen* (armed intruders, many of them farmers desperate to get back to their lands).

However, everyone knew that these were few and far between and only affected the southernmost and northern-most borders, not any centres of population. It made no sense not to allow Arab–Israeli citizens to travel freely, not to give them access to health, education and other services in any comparable measure to that of Israeli Jews and to restrict their entry into a whole range of studies and professions, not to mention into trade unions.

Some of these issues have now been addressed but many still hold true and today there is the added danger of the "Judaisation" of the Galilee, for instance, as well as more recently in the Negev, with old villages and settlements being expropriated and their inhabitants transferred against their will. Today we are told that these villages and settlements had never been officially recognised and hence had never had electricity, water or road access installed. At the time, nobody, at least outside government, had ever heard of unrecognised villages.

Only recently I learned that Israeli citizens have different nationalities: Jewish, Arab or Druze (a small minority who are Arabs but with a slightly different religion), with full rights and benefits only accorded to the first group: discrimination from cradle to grave. My Arab neighbour, although always courteous and welcoming, was reticent to speak of what for her must have been very painful recent events. She was even reluctant to reveal the circumstances of her husband's death.

All she told me was that following it, she had decided to move to the second property that the family owned, no doubt for financial reasons. At least she could get by on the rents paid to her. But sadly she didn't quite trust me. When we emigrated for good in 1958, I suggested she could correspond with her son via us in England. She fell silent. I can't blame her for being wary of us.

Next to our house was a field and off it, set back a little, stood another house in which Karl and Mop (real name Beirute) Stern lived. Karl had been a friend of Ernest since their adolescence in Haifa and we still were quite close although Mop was amazingly self-satisfied for no discernible reason. She was even lazier than me and her home was a thorough mess. She never seemed to suffer from guilt or regrets even when, eventually, in the 1990s, she divorced Karl, having run out of patience with him; according to her, this led to him drinking himself to death. Their daughters, Vera and later Dana, were not very happy when I knew them, either.

Karl was an only child of an adoring Mother and totally incapable of coping with the realities of life. He was intelligent, talented in photography, very well read and cultured, yet he never worked except as an amateur and that infrequently. He was so full of self-doubts and a deep-seated conviction of complete inadequacy that he depended totally on Mop.

Chapter Nineteen

The Sterns helped me and took care of me when I ended up in the A&E department in hospital during a visit in the early seventies, not very long after my divorce. When I told them about it and about Ernest's constant infidelities, Karl confirmed what I had suspected at the time: they had started when I was expecting our first child.

Ending up in the A&E department came about because, during one of my visits, in Jerusalem, I fell ill one night: I couldn't stop vomiting and simultaneously weeping. Early next morning I phoned Mop, who came to drive me to her GP. The latter decided that I needed to get to an A&E department immediately, mainly because I was completely dehydrated. I was put on a drip.

The nurses, concerned about my ceaseless sobbing asked, "Mrs Braun, what's upsetting you so much?"

"I'm so worried about my children," I wept.

"Where are the children?" they asked, by now quite anxious themselves.

"One is in England and the other one in Colombia," I sobbed.

"Mrs Braun, they'll be much more worried about you," they comforted me once they realised that my children were adults.

The strange thing was that, in reality, I was very worried about Smadar, but felt this would be so unfair. It would make me feel biased towards one of my daughters, although I knew this was not the case. I could not explain my deep anxiety regarding only Smadar and so I pretended to myself that I was equally anxious about both of them.

That evening, after various tests, I was discharged and spent a few days at the Sterns' apartment, where the whole affair seemed so ludicrous in retrospect that I literally couldn't stop laughing: an early example of the bi-polar condition that has shaped much of my adult life. I only wish I had been diagnosed much earlier rather than at the ripe old age of 76. Was I born with the condition? Were there earlier manifestations? Modern research tends to regard the condition as non-genetic. More likely, I now think, was my inability to come to terms with the difficulty of two fathers, three name changes and all the problems that ensued from this.

When I finally returned home, a letter from Smadar was waiting for me. She had split in a very painful way from Tim, on the very day I had been taken so ill. I don't believe in telepathy, but this had been a very strange coincidence.

Later I learned to recognise the symptoms of Ernest's infidelities immediately: he would ensure that I knew about the woman in question and would talk about her, pretending that there was nothing going on, yet his tone of voice and his face revealed only too clearly that this wasn't the case. It was almost as if he wished to make sure, with his slightly embarrassed tone and expression, that I at least guessed at the truth.

✧

We decided that for the birth of my first child I should return home and so, about three weeks prior to the expected date, we moved to Haifa, where I stayed at my parents' apartment and Ernest came for the weekends. We arrived in the midst of a strong heat-wave that always felt worse in Haifa than in Jerusalem, the latter having a very dry climate unlike Haifa.

On the earliest date we were expecting Smadar, Ernest came to stay and she arrived promptly one day later than our calculations, on 20th July 1953. It was a very speedy delivery in a maternity home on Mount Carmel. We took a taxi at around seven in the morning as my waters had broken. When we arrived, the nurse who examined me and assured us that it would be several hours yet, we agreed that Ernest would phone at around ten o'clock and later also bring me some reading material I had forgotten. He was amazed to hear that at 9.50 he had become the father of a little girl.

If I had been in any doubt as to whether I had any maternal feelings, they were swept away as soon as she was put in my arms. A great sob came from deep inside me, and a feeling of unbounded love and protectiveness swept over me. My mother came to visit me daily and I was sharply aware of how tired she seemed. At the time, the normal stay after childbirth was a week and after a few days I mentioned to her that she didn't have to visit daily.

"Do I look that bad?" she asked. I assured her that she just looked tired and the bus journey was cumbersome and lengthy. I didn't mention my anxiety about her state of health although even then I didn't realise how close to death she was.

My mother-in-law also had taken to daily visits and I had difficult arguments with her regarding the baby's name. We had agreed on Smadar's first name with some difficulty: both Ernest and his Mother insisted on a name that would be easily pronounceable in European languages, whereas I was keen on a more Eastern name. But when it came to her middle name, my mother-in-law dug her heels in even more than her son: I wanted it to be Paula, after my grandmother, who had died in Terezin (Theresienstadt) concentration camp. I also knew that it was important to my mother, although she tried not to put any pressure on me. I could not and cannot understand why Ernest's mother made it really awkward. She came up repeatedly with different rationalisations, the most disturbing one being that her own mother had died when she bore her first daughter and that she hadn't been in the least interested in naming the child after her, indeed she had never bothered to visit her grave at all.

On this occasion, I stood my ground and Smadar became Smadar Paula, despite grumbles from Ernest and his mother.

Meanwhile, Ernest stayed until I returned to my parents' home, but shortly after that went back to Jerusalem with his mother who was going to look after him once she had bathed "her" baby.

Was her son in need of looking after more than her husband? In my mother-in-law's view, definitely. After all, this was the woman who had left her husband for the best part of a year twice and her older daughter once: on the first occasion, so the baby would be born in Vienna, her hometown, and the second time, so that her son would spend his first school year there.

I remember one letter in particular which upset me greatly: Ernest sounded as if he and his mummy were having a wonderful time and he was certainly not missing me, what with her cooking him all his favourite dishes.

I was vulnerable after Smadar's birth, as well as anxious. About Mother, about my baby, was I doing the right thing in the way I held her, bathed her, fed her? And now I was anxious about my relationship with my husband as well.

Before realising I was pregnant, I had enrolled at the Hebrew University to fulfil my long standing dream of studying there, but once it became clear that my end of year exams would coincide with the birth of my first child, I gave up on it and decided to find a teaching post. I had a very pleasant interview with the head of a school, but spoiled it all by mentioning that I was pregnant even though the baby wasn't due until the middle of the schools' summer holidays.

The headmaster, whose wife had had a very difficult pregnancy that had forced her to spend months horizontally, immediately withdrew his offer. After this, I stopped trying, secretly relieved that I didn't have to teach for the foreseeable future.

And so I stayed home, looking after first Smadar and later our second, Yael, as well, for almost nine years, by which time we were living in Dundee in Scotland. But these years of being mother and housewife were to a large extent years of discontent and boredom, frequently also of misery.

When we returned to my parents' apartment, I was so full of anxieties that I could not relax and enjoy my new baby. When she cried during the night, I became frantic, convinced that something was badly wrong with her. I was also increasingly anxious about my mother's health, which seemed to worsen by the day. She looked so tired! One evening, when she was sitting on the veranda sewing buttons on the baby's blanket, I urged her:

"Mother, go to bed! You look really tired and worn out."

"I want to do at least something for Smadar," she replied.

"It's more important for you to be strong and well enough to play with your little granddaughter when the time comes," was my reply.

Mother said quietly, "I shan't be around for that anyway."

My disquiet mounted, yet I didn't realise that within days I would lose her. In the midst of all this, the military police came trudging up to our apartment to arrest me, due to one of these wonderfully idiotic bureaucratic muddles: in Israel everybody, after completing their three years' military service, is still obliged to go on reserve duty for a month every year, until the age of forty five. As to women, they are exempt once they are three months pregnant. All the documents I had obtained from our GP and sent off in good time had somehow been lost, but when I appeared at the door with a baby in my arms they trooped down again in embarrassment.

I had come home to my parents on 29th July and on 2nd August Mother became severely ill and collapsed with pain in the toilet, from which Julius and I lifted her to her bed. A doctor was called, but he could do little for her. Mother's situation worsened on the 5th and she fell into a coma. This time the doctor explained that she was dying.

With Smadar in my arms, I sat by her bedside and called out to her repeatedly and with increasing urgency. Eventually, she opened her eyes for a split second, recognised the baby and me with a faint flicker of a smile and relapsed into the coma. Later that evening the death rattle started. Aunt Rechi and I frantically urged Julius, who thought she was just sleeping, to recall the doctor. While he was gone, Mother suddenly sat bolt upright, a stream of brown liquid pouring forth from her mouth, fell back again and died.

I was devastated, although at the time, I hurriedly helped my aunt to clear up the mess and tidy the bed. Mother had died sixteen days after Smadar's birth. The following days and weeks were a blur of pain and anxiety. I could not weep, which probably would have helped. A great deal of my milk dried up and I was aware and frantic with anxiety about Smadar's almost constant crying with hunger.

At the time, breast feeding rules were very strict: no feeding for four hours on the dot, no supplementary bottle feeding and no picking the baby up just because it was crying. It took a lot of persistence and persuasion from my side for the nurse to see that Smadar wasn't gaining weight and to agree to supplementary bottle-feeding. Once she started receiving plenty of food, she became well rounded and quite content, and I could at least relax a little.

During this time a letter from Deta arrived: she had some-how managed to obtain our address via the Rachwalskys in England. She wrote to my Mother, enquiring about me and speaking of her experiences during the war. She had finally taken a post with a physician and his family who were equally unhappy with Hitler's regime and they spent all the war years in Denmark.

My reply to her was cruel.

"Dear Marta," I wrote, "Your letter arrived too late. Mother died less than a week ago. Although I feel devastated, having had a baby sixteen days before her death, you are also too late regarding my contact with you. I have become proud to be an Israeli national and do not wish to have any contact with Germans."

I never heard from Deta again and to this day I bitterly regret my arrogance and cruelty, which must have hurt her deeply.

Two weeks after Mother's death, we returned to Jerusalem with Julius, who was incapable of coping alone for at least some weeks. He had been badly shaken by Mother's death, especially as he hadn't recognised how ill she was.

Julius stayed with us for about three weeks, but soon made a remarkable recovery and became his normal self again. He returned home in the company of one of his brothers and a year later was set on marrying a widow of Hungarian descent like him.

After his return to Haifa, I moped about, constantly tired and depressed, until one day Ernest decided to enrol me with the best teacher of Contemporary Dance in Jerusalem, Elsa Dublon, and took me to the first class. Slowly I regained some of my former liveliness and started being more outgoing. And as ever, I escaped into books to relieve the tedium of housekeeping, which I never enjoyed.

The laundry of nappies involved lengthy heating to boiling point on an inefficient old paraffin stove prior to hand washing everything. Cleaning was another chore I much disliked and even washing the floors was not enjoyable. In the Middle Eastern climate, and especially with a young baby, these chores were daily ones and even the help of a sturdy peasant woman from Beit Safafa once or twice a week did little to alleviate my dislike.

Our *falahiyya* (I no longer remember her name) was strong not only physically. It was plain that she was the decision maker in her family. Occasionally, she would also bring the most delicious fresh fruit and vegetables from the family plot to sell. I still remember the figs, apricots, askeduniyas (loquats), salad leaves and herbs she sold us at very modest prices. Nowadays Beit Safafa has become not so much a village, but more of an endangered neighbourhood near Jerusalem, almost unnoticeable due to being cut and isolated by an urban highway near the city's industrial zone in Talpiot.

Chapter Twenty

Even before we married, Ernest, who, unlike me, had never taken to Palestine or to the Middle East in general, claimed that before too long we'd go to Europe. At the time, many young people were talking about this, having been cut off so comprehensively by the war, but only a few actually managed it. It was financially far too difficult. I took his claim with a pinch of salt and believed that he was just another dreamer.

I was wrong. After just two years at the Hebrew University, he managed to persuade the head of the Physics department to send him for two years to Bristol University in England. His mother had persuaded him that, if at all possible, we should opt for Bristol, since his sister with her husband and two young children lived there.

Herta, his older sister, had been sent to a private boarding school in England, shortly before the outbreak of war, with the rest of the family planning to follow, once my father-in-law and his brother, Fritz, had wound up the brewery business. The war overtook them. German troops entered Czechoslovakia and my father-in-law was imprisoned. He managed to buy his way out after a couple of months, but by then, war had broken out and they couldn't emigrate to Britain any longer. The only two choices were China or Palestine. They opted for the latter since it didn't seem quite so remote.

Herta was stranded. Her school fees stopped and she had been forced to leave. After some manual labour, she managed to train as a nurse and eventually, with a will of steel, managed to receive a grant to study medicine in Scotland, at a time when it was still relatively rare for women to get into medical schools in Britain. But the experience had left deep scars. She had been the one who, from early childhood, had always felt excluded from the maternal love that had been lavished on her little brother and, despite the very real reason on this occasion, she couldn't help feeling that yet again she had been abandoned to her fate. She eventually married a Slovak Jew, the only one of his family to escape the Nazis and make it to Britain. Her husband, also Ernest, had fought with the Czech Free army and had been badly wounded in France. Subsequently, he too was given a grant to study medicine in England.

It was not a happy marriage. Herta felt very superior to her husband, who was from a lower middle class background, not to mention that he was "only" a Slovak, that is inferior in development to the much more industrialised Czechs. She made no bones about her feelings. When I first met her, she struck me as very cold and repressive by nature. It was many years before I understood fully how she had become like this: she had erected an inner safety wall to shield her from the hurt that others can cause you if you let them get too close.

Sadly, she continued the prejudices she had experienced as a child. She was extremely cold and unloving towards her oldest daughter, Helen, and, in turn, lavished all her love on the new baby boy, Peter. Her husband was very aware of and unhappy about the situation, but felt powerless to do anything.

Chapter Twenty-one

When we arrived in Bristol in 1954, rationing had just come to an end in Britain and we gorged on biscuits, chocolate and sweets, with foreseeable results to my figure. Ernest didn't seem to be affected by it. As to meat, I had to learn what different cuts and kinds of meat meant, having for some years been restricted to one kilogram of poor quality minced beef. (The better cuts went to the black market). That was the ration per person per month, plus one small chicken during pregnancy.

Another curiosity was the high price of citrus fruit. I had been used to buy it by the kilo, whereas luxuries like apples were bought singly, if at all. In this country, it was the opposite and it took a while to readjust. Last but not least, there were the peculiar dietary and lifestyle habits of the English: potatoes daily, with rice only for puddings, tasteless vegetables boiled to death, very little fruit and salads and endless cups of horrible milky tea.

As to living conditions, hardly anybody used electric or paraffin stoves, let alone central heating, which was practically unheard of. People used to get up in their icy bedrooms and then proceed to build a very smoky and inefficient coal fire in their living rooms, but not elsewhere. Standards of hygiene also appeared to be pretty low. It was only in the late seventies that these began to change among the bulk of the population. The upper classes may have been different and this was another peculiarity: the strict class system and the snobbishness that went with it.

Most people were also openly racist at the time, with placards/leaflets about rooms to let, openly stating "No Blacks, No Irish". To a lesser degree, there was also prejudice against all foreigners. This went hand in hand with a marked ignorance of the geography of anywhere outside Britain and of different languages. No doubt because of the long years of Empire, the English expected everyone else to speak their language, but took little trouble to learn any others. The poor standard of foreign language teaching in British schools continues to these days, when learning a foreign language has ceased to be compulsory beyond the age of fourteen.

Not long after we had settled in our flat, a pleasant though cold apartment in an eight flat house, with the owners living in the ground floor garden flat, I met and became friends with a French–Canadian young woman whose husband, like me, originated from Berlin. We had met in a contemporary dance class run by a lecturer's wife at Bristol University, where George Brandt, Toni's husband, was head of the Drama Department. He had arrived in England with his widowed mother shortly before the outbreak of war, but once the war started they were transported hence to Canada as "undesirable aliens".

George, a highly intelligent and dynamic man, was studying in Canada when he met his future wife, who was from a French Catholic family, but an atheist like him and like us.

At the end of the war, they were able to return and to acquire British nationality. They had a little boy, Peter, who was Smadar's age, and the two of them often played happily together. On one occasion, Smadar, who at the time was barely three years old, and Peter kept pretending they were going shopping for us. Suddenly Peter burst into the room.

"Smadar has gone out. She went through the window!"

I rushed into Smadar's room. The window was closed and even in my panic I couldn't quite see anyone jumping from a window and closing it behind them, but our front door had a lot of decorative glass. I ran into the street and there she was. Although it was dark, I could see her just about to cross the road. When I caught up with her, she burst into tears. Probably she herself was anxious about what she was doing. Like mother, like daughter, although she was even younger than I had been in Berlin.

Not long before this, Smadar had an infection for which Herta's Ernest prescribed antibiotics. At the time, you had to take a tablet every four hours including night times. When I woke her and put her on her potty, she was moaning and whining.

"Never mind," I tried to comfort her.

"My mind isn't in me at all!" she moaned.

Our friendship with the Brandts continued after we returned to Jerusalem and again when we came to Britain for good, but with our frequent moves around Britain (we moved every two or three years following Ernest's promotions at a number of universities) we eventually lost touch. I believe Toni was the first person in this country to ask me outright where I came from. Not only that, she actually knew where Israel was.

The usual response when I announced, still proudly at that time, that I came from Israel, drew blank faces. When I tried to explain that it had until recently been Palestine, I drew more blanks. Eventually I used to fall back on Jerusalem, but even then people would often counter with great surprise that they had believed this city existed only in the bible.

It was Toni too who alerted me to the possibility of anti-Semitism. When I told her one day that the neighbours above us seemed quite hostile to me for no apparent reason, she immediately said, "Maybe they are anti-Semitic."

I was amazed.

"That would never have occurred to me," I replied.

Toni replied that it was the first thing that would occur to her.

My upbringing in Palestine had been good for something after all: to this day, I rarely suspect anti-Semitism, unless it is spelt out and even then I regard it as the anti-Semitic person's problem rather than mine. However, once I recognise it, I don't let it pass any more than I'd let any racist remark pass, with the added benefit that on such occasions I take great pleasure in announcing that I'm Jewish and watching the offenders squirm in embarrassment. Again, a completely different attitude from that of Ernest, who doesn't comment on anti-Semitic remarks, since he claims that he doesn't regard himself as a Jew.

During our stay in Bristol, we were initially welcomed by the Jewish community and were invited to dinner at professor Jaffe's home one Friday evening. But when we confirmed that we never attended synagogue, not even on the highest holidays, which are New Year's Day and the Day of Atonement, he stopped speaking to us and the whole evening became deeply embarrassing. Nevertheless, I gave Hebrew lessons to an evening class of interested people and we also made a few friends, amongst them Karin Blom, the nicest and kindest person one could ever hope to meet. She eventually moved to Israel and we lost touch.

Julius came to visit us in Bristol with the widow and her teenage daughter. By that time, he had become financially well off. He had received generous compensation from Siemens as well as from Mother's and Omi's apartments. He phoned from the railway station to tell us he had arrived, but not to bother, he would take a taxi. The widow and her daughter were staying elsewhere with relatives. Ernest, still unaware of Julius' characteristic behaviour, took him at his word despite my warning. As a result, he was most offended and sulked.

As to marrying the widow, nothing came of it, since the daughter objected strongly to Julius and, I suspect, the mother had her own doubts. I was gratified by the daughter's reaction to him. She had a choice, which hadn't been open to me.

Eventually, not long after this, Julius married another Hungarian, much younger than him. Piri was a very robust, strong woman with limited interest in anything except shopping and accumulating things. She had been a Kapo in a concentration camp and I could well imagine her being brutal. Julius once told me he had hesitated regarding this marriage, but that she had wept and he gave in.

"She isn't like your mother," he once sadly observed.

For me, these first two years in England (1954–1956) were fascinating, but also off-putting: quite apart from the endless rain and grey skies, which made me feel pretty miserable, people at that time were incredibly insular and parochial. It was bearable for two years, but it was clear to me that I would hate to live there permanently. Ernest, on the other hand, relished the English characteristics of rectitude and reserve. He didn't see it as cold and distant. In many ways, his temperament corresponded to that of the typical Englishman of that time: reserved, reticent and totally non-impulsive.

He would often criticise my impulsive nature and my open curiosity towards all others.

"You'll talk to anybody," he would complain.

He was quite correct and this curiosity has remained with me throughout life: I talk to strangers on buses, on the tube and in shops, trying to find out where they hail from and what their mother tongue is. I've become something of an expert at recognising different features and accents. This guessing game about others had started long ago in Palestine: just walking down the street you could see who was Eastern or Central European, who was an English (Jew), Sephardi, Yemeni, Arab (Jew, Muslim or Christian) and so forth.

It is part and parcel of my multi-layered perception of myself: an endless mix, impossible to categorise. In England nowadays, the mix is even wider, especially in the poorer areas of large cities, and there are more possibilities to speculate and to ask people outright.

Chapter Twenty-two

Soon after our return to Jerusalem in 1956 I became pregnant again. Smadar started attending a kindergarten and became great friends with Anat, who was a fortnight older than her. I made friends with her mother, Rahel, a striking-looking, warm and intelligent Egyptian, who had married Hayim Saragusti from a Sephardi family who had been living in the old city. Hayim was an electrician, Rahel a nursery teacher and, I always thought, far more intelligent than her husband. They lived in the German colony, not very far from us and close to the kindergarten. At that time, her mother still lived with the family: a pleasant lady and also good looking.

One lunch time as I collected Smadar from the kindergarten, her teacher asked me:

"Is your husband really a cleaner?"

I was baffled.

"He's a lecturer, why?"

"Smadar always insists that her daddy is a cleaner, who keeps the whole university clean, but he doesn't look or speak like one."

My mistake. Frequently, when we came across street-sweepers or other workmen, I would point out: "Look Smadar, these are workers. They work hard."

I also applied the words to myself. At times, when Smadar wanted something or other, I'd say, "Not now, Smadar, I'm working. Maybe later."

After I once took her to the university to visit her father, and Ernest appeared out of a darkroom in which he was conducting an experiment and then halfway through our visit disappeared momentarily to check on it, Smadar changed her mind regarding Ernest's work completely.

"My daddy works at the university," she would explain proudly, "he plays hide and seek."

Rahel and I became pregnant simultaneously and our second babies were born fourteen hours apart. She was just leaving hospital as I came in. Yael was born even more quickly than Smadar and, on this occasion, my mother-in-law didn't try to interfere when I named her Sella after my mother, as her middle name. In Jerusalem, however, Ernest had an endless and unpleasant argument when registering Yael: he insisted that religion be left blank, explaining she could choose for herself when she grew up. And even in the supposedly secular hospital (since it was a teaching hospital), the professor who had overseen the birth came round a day later to ask me, "I hear you already have a child at home, is it a boy or a girl?"

"A girl," I answered.

"So we'll see you again."

"No, we wanted two children and now we have two."

"But doesn't your husband insist on a boy?"

"Not at all," was my response and he went off, shaking his head.

In religious terms, only male offspring are entitled to say the prayer for the dead at funerals and anniversaries. Females are considered a lesser species and therefore not permitted to participate in numerous activities. And they say Islam is sexist!

With Smadar, it had been far easier to insist religion be left blank, Haifa being a more progressive city. Ernest succeeded in the end and so we are now a completely godless family, both my daughters and my grandsons never having felt the slightest religious inclination.

Sadly, the friendship between Anat and Smadar didn't continue in their younger siblings: they evidently didn't see eye to eye, or rather nappy to nappy.

When Rahel brought along her little Yossi and we placed him in Yael's playpen, he started crying inconsolably while Yael crawled to one corner looking visibly perturbed.

At the time, there was still a pork butcher in what was Mamillah Road. He was a non-Jewish Pole and farmed his pigs outside Jerusalem, but every so often he would end up in prison. There used to be long queues snaking into the street and his wife, who was Jewish, would explain smilingly that her husband was imprisoned again. It must have been well worth their while.

Many years later, in Zimbabwe, in the 1980s, I heard about Anat from a Palestinian Jew, a delegate of the PLO to the Socialist Internationale. The PLO ambassador to Zimbabwe, Ali Halimeh, had invited him as well as me to come and meet him too. Ilan Halevi was outstandingly intelligent, fluent in five languages and a good writer and speaker.

It was Ilan who told me about Anat. She had become a photojournalist and had exposed the truth about two Palestinians who had planned an explosion on some Israeli military target, but were caught on the coach and taken off by Israeli soldiers. The official line was that they had died on the coach or shortly after being hauled off it, due to sickness. Anat had taken the shots of them being led away in perfect health. No Israeli newspaper agreed to publicise the shots, but eventually an American paper did.

In autumn 1956, the Suez crisis erupted and the majority of Israelis were jubilant, whereas Ernest and I were highly critical. I believe that Rahel was equally critical, but she didn't want to talk about it too much, since her husband supported this crazy and immoral adventure. We voiced our condemnation openly: on the morning after the event, I met an acquaintance in the street and told her of my anger at the immorality of the whole event.

"Shush! Not so loud!" she whispered.

When I continued to speak about my dismay, she said, "Well, let's wait and see whether it's going to be successful!"

"What you're saying means that bank robbers can be forgiven provided they manage to get away with the loot?" I responded angrily.

The result of our outspokenness was that we were largely ostracised. Shortly afterwards our postman, a graduate of Madras University, rang our bell very early one morning to inform us in a frightened whisper that all our mail was being opened.

During this time, Ernest was already trying to find a post at Bristol University and in 1958 was invited as research fellow.

It was not what I wanted. I had disliked England during our first visit and the idea of living permanently in that country filled me with dismay. At the time, I didn't want to leave Israel. Although I had become highly critical of its policies, I still loved the country and believed that Zionism had lost its way and that it was up to progressive people to return to the original, socialist ideal.

Moreover, I feared that Ernest's infidelities were likely to continue and that in England I would have no friends or family to turn to if things went wrong. However, Ernest was the breadwinner and therefore the decision maker. Throughout our marriage, I felt I had to accept his decisions regarding holidays, homes and a host of other matters. The trouble was that I was by nature not given to be obedient and so I followed his decisions, but grudgingly and with ill grace.

Shortly before we left, I had another strange encounter with Jewish regulations. Our crates were all packed and ready and a customs officer came to examine them. He didn't really look at anything, just smiled and asked, "No silver or gold, I trust?"

Like a total idiot, I replied that our cutlery was made of silver. This had been a case of "Let them eat cake". When we married, we had been so short of money that both sets of parents helped out and let us have some of their original cutlery. The customs official looked dismayed and told me that he couldn't give us the seal of approval, unless we made a declaration in front of a judge that the cutlery was entirely for personal use and not for sale. According to him, this procedure would take about two months. The transporters were due in two days' time. In panic, I rang the mother of another of Smadar's kindergarten friends whose husband was a judge. She phoned back shortly afterwards and told me to come to the Court immediately and that her husband would see me.

A friend from Tel Aviv had come to visit and I left Yael in her care and set off. Initially I was taken to a large reception room, where an official asked me whether I was religious.

"No, I am not," I stated firmly.

He started dictating. There were the usual bureaucratic questions: name, maiden name, date of birth, address and then: "I swear by God..."

I looked up in surprise.

"I'm not religious," I insisted.

"That's right," said the official and repeated the phrase.

Neither of us could make any sense of the other, until another official, who was sitting at the end of the room, came over and offered to help.

This official was wearing a *kippah,* a rarity at the time. He turned to me.

"You are not religious," he stated.

"No!" I replied despairingly.

"But do you believe in God?"

"No."

"Well, it's all wrong then," said the first official impatiently, tore up the form and made me start from scratch. This time round I had to write: "I, Hanna Braun... swear by my honour because of my lack of belief in God..." This recurred two or three times on the form and when I finally made it to the judge he was not best pleased. I had wasted most of his lunch hour. The clerk with the *kippah* enlightened me on my way out: according to biblical laws, you should not use the name of the lord in vain and silver cutlery definitely falls into this category.

Chapter Twenty-three

When we arrived in England, a dockworkers' strike was in full swing and it took almost a year for us to be reunited with our crates. Herta had lent us most essentials, but it was still a lovely surprise to unpack all the books, records, photo albums and other possessions we had all but forgotten about. On this second occasion, our old apartment was occupied and we ended up in an apartment that was less self-contained. There was a shared entrance door and staircase with the owners, a sour-faced elderly widow, her even more sour-faced unmarried daughter and an adopted boy, himself quite disturbed and difficult.

The daughter had converted from the Anglican to the Roman Catholic Church, which was why she was allowed to adopt the boy even though she was unmarried and well into middle age and the boy was already three years old. Mother and daughter were some of the most bigoted, narrow-minded and fervently religious people I'd ever come across and our stay in the apartment was not a happy one. I made the mistake of revealing quite early on that we were non-believers and this horrified them completely.

When Paul Robeson came to perform in Bristol, tickets went very fast. I offered to buy an extra ticket for the daughter, but was rebuffed with her telling me disapprovingly that she didn't wish to waste time on listening to his "ditties". Smadar was only five years, old but we took her along. To us it was a wonderful and unforgettable evening.

In 1961, I finally went to visit Manfred/Pappi in Munich, where he had ended up as Emeritus Professor, although the details of this are somewhat murky. He had never been employed by Munich University and must have spun some of his highly imaginative tales to obtain this title. Prior to my visit, his secretary had urged me repeatedly to come, as he wanted so much to see me.

At the time, the most common travel was still by ferry and rail. The railway carriage on the train to Munich was filled with well-fed Germans. At that time they made my skin crawl and I shrank into myself as much as possible. A kindly conductor noticed my discomfort and told me there was a Jewish gentleman two carriages down.

I made my way and sat down. Gentleman, my foot! He was one of the black marketeers who had sprung up after the war. Normally, he would give me the creeps too. But I remembered the response of Fritz Lang, the famous German–Jewish film director who, when students complained to him that although they had the greatest admiration and respect for him, they loathed the Jewish black marketeers:

"Forgive us our black marketeers and we'll forgive you your murderers."

Once I was in Pappi's apartment, I was deeply shocked. He was a bedridden wreck of a man, with an air of gloom about him. I would never have recognised him. The main reason for the secretary's urgings also became apparent: a young, good-looking woman was embedded as his companion/carer and the secretary was convinced that she was simply after his inheritance. The companion, Marianne, took me around to show me the sights of Munich and was quite pleasant, but when her boyfriend came round to visit, it was I who became aggressive and unpleasant. He was a minor aristocrat who'd served in the German air force during WWII and to me this meant he was a Nazi, despite his protests. When he observed that he would like to see Israel, I said aggressively,

"You wouldn't be allowed in." At the time, I was still so much the typical, arrogant Israeli. It took many years for me to lose this attitude.

When shortly after the end of the war Yehudi Menuhin had given a concert in Germany, I could not comprehend the great humanity and generosity of his action and thought of it almost as betrayal.

What was worse was that my attitude to Manfred wasn't much better. I couldn't understand how anyone could return to live in Germany, let alone pretend that the name *Fraenkel* came originally from the Huguenots. With hindsight, his options were limited: in his early eighties and with a shadow of suspicion of collaboration hanging over him, there wasn't much else he could do.

I still have the memory etched in my mind of him crying helplessly in his bed as I was leaving without even embracing or kissing him. Why was I so harsh and ungenerous?

He died not long after my visit. All our correspondence, as well as some photos, were sent to me in Birmingham, where I lived with my husband and daughters at the time. All of them are now yellowing amongst my papers and I haven't the heart to throw them out. In one of the first letters after we learned he was still alive he asked, "Does Lilo know?" Mother's reply was somewhat ambiguous, "She does and she doesn't. She refused to accept the idea; we had some very difficult times." What an understatement!

Among the letters preserved by Pappi and forwarded to me after his death, I found one written in 1939. It speaks for itself:

"My beloved Pappi!

I wish you a happy birthday and all things good and pleasant with all my heart. May you live long, remain healthy and have no worries. You know how much I love you and how I'd love to be with you. Although not this birthday, I'm certain that we'll meet many times in the future. My warmest thanks for the beautiful books. *Tom Sawyer* has arrived and I've read some of it already and as to *The Last Days of Pompey* about which I read in your dear card, for which all my heartfelt thanks, it's sure to arrive shortly. Enjoy your birthday, as I did mine, and don't forget us, just as we, dear Mother and I, won't forget you.

Many kisses and congratulations from your loving daughter, Lilo."

On the back of my letter was Mother's, possibly even more revealing:

"Dearest, warmest congratulations from me as well!

The child – she's twelve now – was really pleased with the book, which arrived today together with your kind card. On her birthday she said immediately, "Nothing from Pappi. It's the first time he's forgotten." Now she's proud that this wasn't so. She continues to develop well, is free and feels very nationalistic ... Recha and Paul aren't altogether happy.

Acclimatisation is difficult for all of us. Our greatest worry is Mother (my grandmother). She's completely on her own now, had to leave her apartment and move in with a friend. Unfortunately they have to move from there as well and with conditions as they are today they can't find anything. We're trying hard to obtain a permit for her and haven't achieved anything. How much longer is she going to be able to travel?

Take good care of yourself.

Warm hugs and kisses from your

Sella"

Chapter Twenty-four

Our first journey to England was by boat; this time we flew. Following this, Smadar told anyone who was interested, as well as various people who were definitely not, "There is no God. I looked."

She had started infant school and had also completely forgotten Hebrew. When we arrived in Bristol in summer 1958, she had such an atrocious Hebrew accent when speaking English that I decided to speak only English with her until she started school, lest her new classmates made fun of her. Even before the first term started, she received a postcard in Hebrew from a kindergarten friend. When I read it to her, it dawned on me that she didn't understand a single word. Still, her logic was outstanding. When I collected her from school one day, she told me that she and Margaret, her best friend at school, were exactly the same height.

"How do you know?" I asked.

"Well, Margaret is the same height as Alice and I'm the same as Alice, so that means we're both the same."

I swelled with pride inside myself until I asked her:

"Who's Alice? You've never mentioned her before."

"Alice in Wonderland, of course."

My pride deflated, its balloon punctured.

Around this time, my parents-in-law also arrived in Bristol after my father-in-law's retirement. My mother-in-law had always insisted on England, and specifically Bristol, and so she had her way. My father-in-law followed as usual. He wasn't always in agreement with her, but tended to do as his wife wished without much protest. Herta and her mother had decided that the semi-detached house that they and their family lived in should be extended by buying the other half, and breaking through a connecting door.

Herta's Ernest was not happy with the project. He felt, rightly, that his parents-in-law would be too uncomfortably close but had no say in the matter. From that time onwards, Herta and her mother made all the decisions, including which school Helen, Herta's eldest daughter, should attend. Herta was making up for all the years when she had felt rejected and even abandoned in favour of her younger brother.

As to me, with my mother-in-law's frequent interference, these years were not happy. Almost the only joy I experienced was that of seeing Smadar and Yael developing and growing. It was also a period when I devoured books more hungrily than ever. I used the library endlessly, had them order all of Berthold Brecht's works in German, waded my way through Dickens and grabbed Doris Lessing's books as soon as they appeared.

Quite often, I would walk through the dark streets once the children were in bed, trying to shake off my loneliness and misery. Another act of defiance was my insisting on Ernest stopping the car after one of our frequent arguments. If he refused, I would open the door and thus force him to stop (this was years before seatbelts were common, let alone compulsory). I would again walk aimlessly for a long time before returning home. This led to my mother-in-law spreading rumours about me having affairs. I wish!

After two years in Bristol, we moved to Harlow New Town in Hertfordshire, a recently built town designed to take the overspill from London after the war. Ernest wanted to try out work in an industrial research outfit nearby, but eventually was disappointed and returned to academe. Not all of our time in Harlow was bleak: both children were developing their own characteristics, made friends and often were inadvertently funny. Yael had a special "wee-wee" brook in Epping Forest, where she invariably would insist on crouching and peeing when we went for walks, but there were various other small streams and brooks that took her fancy. At times it felt like walking a dog through a tree-lined street.

She also came up with various stories purporting to show her exemplary innocence and honesty. On one occasion, Ernest and I were working in the garden, when both Yael and Smadar appeared at the window.

"Can we have a sweet?" Yael asked.

I looked up and said, "You know you shouldn't ask for sweets between meals."

"I didn't want to ask," replied Yael, "Smadar made me."

Smadar's mouth fell open and it was obvious what had really occurred.

Yael also waited in the hall for Ernest on one occasion. When he appeared, she started spinning him a long story of how good she'd been and how horrid I'd been to her all day. Half way through her tale, she interrupted herself to ask: "If I ask you not to ask mummy if it's true, does that mean I'm lying?"

126

"Not necessarily," answered Ernest.

"Don't ask mummy!" came her swift reply.

Smadar was doing well at school and enjoying it and eventually Yael started school as well. Smadar started piano lessons and I decided at long last to take lessons as well, from the same teacher. It was evident that he was attracted to me. Over time he moved nearer and nearer to me until we all but embraced. Although I was well aware that Ernest was having yet another of his flings with a secretary who came twice weekly and to whom he'd give a lift home, I didn't feel I could act in a similar manner. For one thing, Mr Fitzpatrick (I've by now forgotten his first name) was married, which to me presented a big taboo.

I couldn't bring myself to let another woman suffer in the way I was, with Ernest's frequent infidelities. And then there were the logistics. Where, when and how, with my daughters in the house? So it came to nothing.

It was Fitzpatrick who soon discovered my uselessness at reading music. He'd put his newspaper in front of the score and remark that in reality it didn't make the slightest difference. Although this showed my very strong ear and memory for music – I managed to play some gavottes as well as easier pieces by Bach and Beethoven – it was also a severe disadvantage. I was aware that once I'd want to tackle longer and more complicated pieces, I'd be lost.

After three years in Harlow, Ernest obtained the post of lecturer at Dundee University in Scotland. So off we went again, settled in one of the University's apartments not far from it and even nearer to Dundee College of Education and its adjacent school, which at the time was the only school in Scotland not to practise corporal punishment.

Once we'd moved from Harlow, I didn't continue with my piano lessons, partly no doubt because of my tendency to start projects without ever finishing them.

When we arrived in Dundee in September, the girls started school immediately. At the time, we created a stir in Dundee to the extent that one of the local papers sent a reporter round to interview me and take photos of me, Smadar and Yael. We'd come from Israel, a marvellously exotic, foreign place!

Scotland is beautiful, but Dundee was downright ugly. For the first part of the year, we travelled around to see the wonderful glens north of the city.

There was nothing in the way of Dance in Dundee, except for ballet or Scottish Dance and so I joined such a class, but didn't really take to it. Scottish dancing, like many other Northern European dances, involves feet only, rather than the whole body and on top of it the almost incessant calls to cast off and on are like nothing so much as knitting.

Another aspect of the city – and probably of Scotland generally – was the tight respectable conformity.

You couldn't be mildly non-conformist. If you stepped out of line, you were regarded as eccentric at best. All this may well have changed now, but I'm thinking of Scotland in the early sixties. As to the very long summer days, I quite liked these although it seemed odd that you could read a newspaper in the street away from streetlights at eleven o'clock at night.

But how I hated the long winter nights! You would leave home at half past eight in the morning and all was still in darkness as it was when you returned around four o'clock or even earlier.

Throughout the year, there was a period of incredibly long twilight, which I also disliked intensely. It was so diametrically the opposite of what I regarded as normal. I used to draw the curtains as soon as the "gloaming" ("glooming" to me) started, while many Scots regarded it as beautiful and romantic. And it was so cold! Once we left the country, I never returned for a visit, no doubt chiefly because of my unhappy experience in it.

Come to think of it, I never returned to visit Birmingham, except for the occasion of Nelson Mandela's pre-election visit, when I came from Coventry with a group of anti-Apartheid activists. The reason was much the same.

People in Airlie Place, mostly academics or students, as well as the square next to it, were friendly and inclusive. Shortly after Christmas, we were invited to a most enjoyable Hogmanay party, but I couldn't help noticing Ernest's quite open flirtation with Isobel, the wife of one of the wealthiest men in Dundee. This soon developed into something far more serious and glaringly obvious than any previous flings had been.

Eventually I confronted Ernest and he assented that he loved Isobel and that our marriage was finished in any case, as I was "too much of a mother and not enough of a wife."

Despite my devastation, which ended with a complete breakdown and a short stay in hospital, I decided to follow the hospital psychiatrist's advice to cut my losses and look forwards, in particular for Smadar and Yael's sake. After a few days I left the hospital, but not before telling Ernest that, since he regarded our marriage as finished, I wanted him to be gone by the time I came home. He complied without protest, probably thinking that his life would be simpler without me around.

The following months were grim. I forced myself to look after my daughters as best I could, simultaneously taking myself in hand. I had gained a lot of weight during the years I'd spent at home, not to mention feeling obliged to eat up all my children's leftovers. Now I gave up sugar and biscuits and the pounds soon started falling off. Curiously, I did this while still struggling to come to terms with no longer smoking.

Shortly before the Isobel saga started, Ernest had announced that he'd never go anywhere with me unless I stopped smoking. I had made numerous attempts since marrying, but with little success: I'd cut down then increase my intake again. In Dundee, though, I decided to stop altogether. When Ernest subsequently took up with a woman who was herself a smoker, I was seriously tempted, but decided that I wasn't giving up for his sake but for my own. Luckily, after the first few months, I no longer felt the need to smoke and haven't smoked since.

How did I get the idea of returning to work? I no longer remember details, but I wrote to my old College of Education and asked them for a translation of my diploma into English. For good measure I also wrote to my old school with the same request. Both arrived in due course, despite being addressed to "Scotland, England". I took them to the local Department of Education, where I was told that I would be recognised as a teacher from England. I needed to take an additional year at the college, for which I would receive a grant. After this, I would be qualified for all of Britain.

Teachers from England were understandably furious about their lack of recognition in Scotland, but for me it was a godsend: not only did I feel out of practice, I had never taught in a British school and expected to gain confidence through this course. In many ways I certainly did.

The course started in September and I took to most of the lecturers and many of the students. There were a few "mature" students, but I tended to feel more remote from them. My greatest enjoyment derived from literature, pedagogy, art and last but not least physical education, during which the tutor asked me on one occasion to lead a session in Contemporary Dance.

Moreover, it was the four hundred year anniversary of Shakespeare's birth, which the department of English celebrated by putting on excerpts of several of his plays. I wanted to be involved but did not see how I would be able to act in what was at the time still a thick German accent. Instead I volunteered to choreograph the 'masque' from the *The Tempest*. The music I chose was from a contemporary of Purcell, whereas the steps and choreography were simple steps and movements I had used many years ago in Palestine/ Israel. It turned out to be a great success, with heart-warming support and applause from audience, dancers and lecturers alike. A great and much needed boost to my self-confidence!

Many years later in London I watched a breathtakingly beautiful Dance Performance by Mark Morris and his company. They danced Milton's *L'Allegro*, *Il Penseroso* and Johnson's additional *Il Moderato*, set to music by Handel. Their style and choreography were totally contemporary, with the latter amazingly close to my interpretation at the college, although far superior as they were professionals. But when I read that Morris had started his career with Balkan Dances the connection became clear.

One of the lecturers, the Psychology one, irritated me to the point that I lost any respect for him. Initially he announced that we should feel free to question him on anything we disagreed with, but as soon as I and a few others took him at his word, he evaded any issue, mainly by claiming there wasn't time for it.

In winter we had the first exam. I knew I had written a good paper but received 57% for it. Even trying to approach the Head of Department was futile. No colleague, even a senior one, would take the side of a student.

When the summer exams came, I wrote what I knew he thought right. On this occasion, I received 82%. He made the mistake of asking me smugly in front of the class what mark I had received the previous time.

"Fifty-seven percent," I answered sullenly.

"You see, you can actually do so much better."

This was too much.

"No," I retorted, "last time I wrote what was right. This time I wrote a lot of rubbish which I knew would give me a good mark."

There was a collective intake of breath from the class and the lecturer went bright red.

"Well, we all have to have our rebels," he said.

What, me, a rebel?

The trouble with my ear resurfaced in 1964 after I completed my additional one-year course at the Dundee College of Education. We had to pass a medical examination prior to receiving our diplomas. The highly unpopular doctor tested my hearing by asking me to go into one corner of the room, facing the wall, and to put a finger in my right ear. She then whispered something that I had to repeat. When she asked me to do the same with my other ear, I stupidly said that I didn't hear in that ear. It hadn't even occurred to me to pretend to put my finger in my left ear and thus save myself a great deal of trouble. The doctor was outraged.

"You've been for a year and you tried to hide it!" she accused me.

I replied that I wasn't hiding anything since I didn't feel I had a hearing problem – to no avail. When I explained that I had three years' teaching experience behind me, not to mention active service in the army, she brushed it all aside.

"I cannot give you a health certificate until I observe you teaching," she declared.

Furiously I decided not to let this happen. I would simply ignore any appointment to teach in front of her. A somewhat older Israeli friend, whom I had met in Dundee, talked sense into me. The college she had attended some years previously would never side with a student against any member of staff.

If I wanted to obtain my diploma and teach, so Shula said, I needed to swallow my pride and to give a lesson observed by the doctor. At the end of this lesson, which had been attended by the doctor and a lecturer, I was most gratified, when on our way out, the lecturer said in front of her that as far he was concerned, the whole exercise was a complete waste of time.

Shula had met and married a Scottish psychiatrist in Palestine while she was studying at the Hebrew University during WWII. They lived in Broughty Ferry on the opposite bank of the Tay.

Ernest would take the girls on Sundays or at times on Saturdays for the day. Occasionally he would take Isobel as well and the two of them would disappear for a while. Only many years later, after I had divorced him, did Smadar divulge this to me. He also took the girls to see their grandparents one Easter holiday and I spent a week or so travelling around the North of Scotland.

I went to places that were so remote at the time that you could walk for hours without meeting anyone, although the occasional passer by invariably greeted me with great courtesy. The Highlands were beautiful and awe inspiring, yet to me they seemed so very desolate places. No doubt they reflected my mood.

This was also the time when Yael showed amazing maternal feelings, although to a large baby doll, Helen. Whenever Ernest took the girls, I would receive detailed orders of when to feed her "baby", when she should sleep etc. I felt almost guilty whenever I entered the girls' room about so totally ignoring Helen. I made up by including her when I started making simple shift dresses for them, mainly for the beach.

Some years later, when we all went on holiday to Italy with Ernest driving, the border guard looked puzzled: "There are only two children entered in the passport," until he realised that the third one was a doll.

The end of Helen's life came when we were on holiday in Slovenia. We made friends with a German–Jewish family from London. Yael, who was nearly eight years old at the time, befriended their daughter, slightly younger than herself. On one occasion the friend wanted to look at something in our girls' room. Yael rushed ahead of her and hid Helen and any items that might reveal her existence. The embarrassment persuaded her that it was time to give up.

That first summer we had initially intended to go for a holiday in Italy as a family. Once we had separated, I decided to go with the girls anyway. I booked a fortnight's holiday in Riccione, an Adriatic resort, at the time still fairly quiet, although there were plenty of tourists even then. Prior to our visit, there had been some cases of typhoid fever in Scotland, and Italy demanded that all potential tourists from the country have typhoid injections prior to entering Italy.

The results were dramatic for us, although I should have known: I used to have very strong reactions every time we had our bi-annual injections at school. As we returned from our GP, initially the girls, and not long afterwards I too, started running very high temperatures with swollen and painful arms where we'd been injected.

"The second injection won't be nearly as bad," I assured them. I was wrong: it was even worse! To add to our ills, I had forgotten the keys and we couldn't get into our flat. I took the girls to a neighbour's flat, phoned the fire brigade and asked them to enter via an open window. I was assured that they'd come as soon as they could.

An hour later, I phoned again. By now, Smadar and Yael were groaning in agony as well as very hot to the touch. The fire fighters were apparently waiting for a police officer. They eventually turned up, policeman in tow, climbed up and opened the door for us. The policeman then asked me some seemingly pointless questions. One of the fire fighters explained that they'd had many similar calls that turned out to have come from burglars who then took whatever they wanted without having to do any strenuous or dangerous climbing. As a result, they were now obliged to be accompanied by a police officer whenever people asked them to open entrance doors or windows for them. I couldn't help but feel a sneaking admiration for the cheek of those burglars.

Our Italian holiday was very pleasant with great swimming. We had arranged that I'd spend the first week alone with the girls, after which Ernest would collect them to spend the second week with him. This was the first time I had a short fling – with a young Swede – as well as being ogled by a few other males. It made a big difference to my morale and I started to feel attractive again.

It was sometime during the second year in Dundee that Ernest, who was supposed to pick up the girls one Sunday, didn't show up. I phoned, but got little joy out of him. He seemed to be unwell. Concerned, I went round to his bed-sit to find him in bed. Isobel had left him and returned to her husband, whom she'd actually never really left, although he was well aware of the situation.

Ernest, as ever, expressed himself in a cliché: "It was not to be."

For the rest of my college year, I didn't wish him to return, but we had more contact than before.

He soon started putting out feelers regarding us getting together again, but I was most uncertain, telling him, "Only if you go to see a marriage councilor first."

He went once, but declared it was a complete waste of time and that he had no intention of going again.

Towards the end of my college year, he asked me to give our marriage another chance and to come with him to London or nearby, since he had been accepted as a reader at West Ham Polytechnic.

I was very reluctant and wary, but still felt that for our daughters' sake it would be better for us to stay together, although I didn't feel very enthusiastic about it.

"I've learned my lesson," claimed Ernest while I was still dithering. But he hadn't.

Eventually I decided to try a compromise: I had set my heart on St. Christopher School in Letchworth Garden City, originally founded by a Quaker, a very progressive independent school that took both boarders and day pupils. It would at least give the girls stability in case of another split and I particularly liked the relaxed, friendly atmosphere, so different from most English schools. It reminded me a bit of my own school in Haifa.

And so we settled on a semi-detached marriage in Letchworth, with Ernest coming for long weekends only. He hated St. Christopher's school. For him it was far too unconventional. I already had a job waiting for me at Baldock Secondary School, now The Knights Templar Comprehensive School.

Among various well-known parents at St. Chris, I encountered Joe Slovo and Ruth First at parents' days. One of their daughters, Gillian, now herself a writer, wrote in the school magazine that when her Mother came home from prison she was just the same as ever. When I read her mother's own account in *117 Days*, it became clear what an iron will and self-control she was capable of.

✧

When Julius and Piri came to visit us in Letchworth we were so concerned as to how to keep her amused, that we bought our first TV set shortly before their arrival. It was a great success when they weren't in London, shopping. Julius had to cart around incredibly heavy bags and suitcases, wheezing loudly. Being a heavy smoker did not help.

At the time, the perils of tobacco were as yet unknown. If Julius contributed to Mother's early death, I have no doubt at all that Piri contributed to his own. And yet Smadar remembers a positive side of her, climbing with some difficulty over nettles and shrubs to gather blackberries for her and Yael. Julius was her third husband and she remarried again after his death. They still came to visit us in Birmingham, but not long after this I stopped corresponding with Julius.

The reason was trivial, but it was the final straw as far as I was concerned: he had sent me an LP with Israeli music. On one side was the great song, "If I were a rich man" from *Fiddler on the Roof*. On the other side was an extremely chauvinistic song. When I wrote to thank him, he asked in his next letter whether I liked the LP. I replied that the first side was lovely. Still not enough. How had I liked the second side?

"Well, since you insist on asking, I didn't like it at all," was my response.

Julius' reply was one of bitter accusations: I was so ungrateful, showing yet again my lack of love towards him. That settled it. I didn't reply and returned a couple of letters he'd sent after this unopened. I heard no more, but one of his brothers phoned me one night to inform me that he had died suddenly from a massive heart attack.

Luckily, in Jewish practice you have to bury the dead within twelve hours, so there was no possibility of me attending the funeral. The uncle gave me all the details of the burial site and I pretended to write them down. Julius had evidently told nobody of the breakdown of our relationship and I didn't want to dig this up now.

Chapter Twenty-five

Baldock, my first teaching post in England, was at that time a small market town with around 6,000 inhabitants; it made up in numbers of pubs for Letchworth which was completely 'dry.' We lived about two miles from the school and I used to walk to it in the mornings then later catch a bus or, frequently, get a lift home.

This was the time when I tried my hand at driving, with spectacular lack of success. My instructress was a chain-smoker who didn't inspire much confidence. I used to be so tense that I never recognised our street when I drove home with her, let alone our house. After a while the instructress claimed I was ready for a test. I registered but chickened out and made some excuse not to go. After the same thing happened again I gave up. What worried me most was that by some fluke of fate I might actually pass the test and as a result would have to drive. I hated this idea!

Mr. Crellin, the headmaster, ran the school on highly traditional and positively puritanical lines: there was strict streaming, not always according to mental ability but sometimes because some of the girls in particular had been seen by Mr. Crellin 'snogging' in the park of an evening or even just chatting to boys across the fence during school breaks. I resolved to introduce some changes so as to give these girls a better chance of self-worth and myself greater enjoyment.

One of the innovations was that on Friday afternoons I was permitted to have one of the girls of the C-stream leavers to come dressed as she would for a job interview, while the rest of the girls would look at her outfit, make up etc. and pass judgement.

They were often more critical than I was. Linda, a very fat girl, came dressed one Friday afternoon in a way that a colleague described as designed for "only one possible job she can have in mind." She was clad in black leather, her jacket studded with gilt knobs, a black mini skirt and high heels. The other girls made such mincemeat of her that I felt quite sorry for her. Linda was near to tears. I commented that black was slimming, the only positive thing I could think of.

On other occasions, I took the girls to different work places: a hospital, a nursery, a hairdresser etc. I also invited some girls who had left the previous year to come and talk about their new working life.

At the end of my first year at Baldock, Ernest was invited as visiting professor to Washington State University for three months and the girls and I came to visit for three weeks. I had to take almost a week off school so that we could still fly out just before Smadar's twelfth birthday and pay only half the fare for her.

Our first stop was New York, where we had booked into a modest hotel near the City Centre. On the first evening two sisters who were relatives of Julius' came to visit us. They had emigrated from Palestine not long after the war. We had used to see them quite often in Tel Aviv, where they lived with their niece, a girl somewhat older than me. Why she went to Palestine without her parents had remained a mystery to me. Had they been early victims of Hitler's regime? Had they been politically involved in underground resistance or Socialism? Nothing was ever said but it was clear that her aunts had little warmth or affection for her. When the aunts moved to the USA, she remained in Palestine and we lost touch.

As to the sisters, the most disturbing thing to me was that they told me they had settled in Brooklyn, but were no longer happy there since "blacks" were moving in. I didn't say anything, but was appalled that they seemed to have learned nothing from the Hitler years.

Our extensive sight-seeing in New York, although the city was fascinating and we managed to include a boat trip, during which you could view practically all the most famous buildings and sky scrapers, didn't endear it to me. It was just too much: too noisy, too boastful, too big with such overpowering skyscrapers, and with everybody too hurried. My most lasting and positive impressions were of the Guggenheim Museum and the Museum of Modern Art. Yael's observation, though, was spot on: "Mummy", she kept saying, "there are THINGS here."

We also visited Washington DC, where old Berlin friends of Mother's, Bob and Dascha, had ended up. From the airport, we took a taxi to their place. I struck up a conversation with our African-American driver, since, as usual, I hate to sit in total silence next to anyone. He went out of his way to point out places and chat to us, in all likelihood because, at the time, the United States was still far more blatantly racist, and not only in the South.

After a long day in Washington DC, we flew to Spokane, the nearest airport to Washington State University, where Ernest met us at the airport and drove us to the pleasant bungalow in Pullman that had been allocated to us by the university.

Long weekends followed. The first was westwards to the Cascade Mountains and Mount Rainier. They were spectacular, with one side of the mountain covered in snow even in the heat of summer, while the other side was lush and green. When we descended from the snow-covered side, Yael simply sat on her behind and slid down. Later that evening, there was an incredible thunderstorm with lightning the like of which I only saw years later in Zimbabwe.

We ended up in Seattle, whence Ernest drove us back to Pullman.

Our second trip was to the Rocky Mountains, close to the Canadian border. We stayed in a log cabin in a National Park and were warned to keep talking or even whistling on our walks, so as not to alarm any bears. We never encountered any, but on one occasion, watched a pair of marmots sunning themselves. The great natural beauty of the place was marred for me by a plague of midges. I scratched incessantly and could hardly stand still to listen to our guide, with whom a group of us had gone on a half-day tour.

On the way back, we drove through Montana. It was getting late and we were hungry. We stopped at a small diner, which turned out to be completely Mexican. The punters, all male, looked mostly sad and forlorn. They kept playing Mexican songs on a jukebox. The owner, also Mexican, couldn't do enough for us: did the girls like their eggs sunny side up, or turned over etc. Yael was so tired her head slumped onto the table.

Later, I overheard the owner telling the punters something about "Lord Ingles" and nodding in our direction.

(The only other time I can recall such a hilarious mala-propism was some years later, when on holiday with Yael in former Yugoslavia. We were in a hotel lift with an American couple. I said something to Yael and the man promptly told his wife, "Poor Aaxford" (pure Oxford). I had to nudge Yael hard to stop her giggling.

When we were leaving, he called Ernest aside to give him a smallish lump of silver for the girls. The men were all miners in the silver mines of Montana.

As to Pullman itself, and by and large what I saw in the United States, I was under-whelmed. The perception of most of the people we came across, especially in the West, was that everything in the States was so much bigger and better than elsewhere. It was certainly bigger, but it drove me to the conclusion that small is beautiful. I also found it difficult to distinguish the young sons and to a lesser degree, daughters of Ernest's colleagues: they all seemed to have round heads with crew cuts emphasizing their thick necks, as well as sausage fingers. Of the many countries I have seen and visited, the USA is one of only two that I would not mind in the least never visiting again. The other one is Turkey.

Shortly before we left, a young man and his wife turned up at our bungalow. The university had appointed him and they were going to live in the place after us. It turned out that they were Egyptians.

"Oh, we're neighbours," I said, explaining that we came from Israel.

"Do you want to fight?" he asked, half joking.

My explanation that we were quite critical of Israel and didn't live there any longer and that I actually had some admiration for President Abd-el Nasser left him dumbfounded.

On our way home to England, we stopped off for another couple of days in New York and, on this occasion, while we were heading for Central Park, we came across Tiffany's. On the spur of the moment, I decided to go in and look around. I was delighted when both Smadar and Yael repeatedly exclaimed within earshot of the elegantly clad male attendants, "Mummy, your jewellery is much nicer!"

Although it was laughable nonsense, my jewellery mostly consisting of lovely, intricate filigree Palestinian pieces, frequently made by Bedouins, i.e. containing only five percent silver, or else of pure brass, it felt great.

Chapter Twenty-six

In September, when school started again, I continued to enjoy my teaching as well as my extra-curricular activities. My relationship with my pupils was good. I introduced a group of them to Contemporary Dance as well as Drama. Initially we concentrated entirely on improvisation, but when a countywide competition in Dance-Drama was announced, we decided to participate, despite the pupils' initial concerns that they weren't "good enough". I reassured them that all the participants would be amateurs and so we proceeded. The group had chosen all the music from a variety of cassettes I'd brought, and settled mainly on Janáček, but the thunderstorm had to be from Beethoven's sixth symphony, the Pastoral.

We practised assiduously and on the evening the group unexpectedly won first prize. After that we continued with our Improvisations and Dances for as long as I worked at the school.

Pupils who had completed O- and A-level exams had a few weeks to wait for the holidays. So as to arouse their interest in various people who influenced, or tried to influence, society, I invited various persons of public standing to a weekly question and answer session on Friday afternoons, with the sessions always chaired by a student.

I particularly remember Shirley Williams, at the time our local Labour MP, and I admired her tact in taking great care to answer questions relating to the election and subsequent work of an MP while avoiding party politics altogether.

On another occasion I had invited an advertising executive about whom the students were initially very excited. He had arrived in a Daimler, they rushed up to tell me! However, they ended up regarding him almost with contempt: after increasingly pointed questioning (this was the era of "*Persil washes whiter than white*"), he admitted that you don't necessarily have to believe everything adverts say.

One student put it succinctly: "So you work for something you don't believe in?"

The executive himself, so smooth and suave, had managed to unmask the lies upon which most advertising is based.

One of the most interesting events during these Fridays was the time I invited a panel consisting of a priest, a vicar, a rabbi and a humanist. It was shortly after the contraceptive pill had become widely available and of course the students' main queries regarded the respective attitudes of the panel members to this innovation. The priest, who was from one of the Cambridge colleges, admitted that he wouldn't prevent young people from using it, albeit reluctantly. The vicar's reply was similar, the humanist had no problems whatsoever, but I was truly shocked by the rabbi's reply: "Actually, not enough Jewish babies are being born!"

Having found out that I originated from Israel, he insisted that we come to a community evening in a private home, the following Saturday.

"I'm afraid we are completely secular, we never go to any Synagogue," I replied.

The Rabbi was adamant.

"That doesn't matter at all," he claimed, "you'll be very welcome."

After our experiences in Bristol, we were very wary, but reluctantly made our way to the home of one of the members of the community. This was shortly after the June 1967 war. We were warmly welcomed and sat down with some twenty other people. The very first thing that happened was someone passing around a collection box and saying "For our boys," meaning Israeli soldiers fighting and winning over Egypt, Jordan and Syria in the Six Day War.

For once, Ernest spoke up:

"We should be collecting for the Palestinian refugees."

There was an icy silence and we were simply frozen out.

That was the last time I got involved with an exclusively Jewish group.

I got on well with most of my colleagues, with some exceptions. As usual, I didn't take well to authority if I didn't think it reasonable, and I had two notable run-ins.

The first case was a minor one. It occurred at the end of the school year, when the deputy headmaster, a Mr Fisher, who had been a Sergeant Major and behaved like one, ordered me to have my pupils clean the desks that had graffiti on them. They did, but I saw no need for them to clean all the desks. Soon afterwards, he stormed into the staff room just as I was leaving it:

"That woman," he fumed, "that woman does what she wants!" The rest of the staff was hugely amused and intrigued.

"What have you been up to now?" they asked.

The next and more serious stand-off occurred in quite a different context. The trouble was a recommended reading list, which I had put up on the wall for my 5th and 6th form pupils. One of the books was *Saturday Night and Sunday Morning*. One boy, who practically never read books, did take to this one, which he borrowed from the school library. His mother promptly marched into Mr Crellin's office and complained about "the filth" her son was reading. Mr Crellin, appalled, asked the new head of the English department to sort it out with me. The original head, Ken Calthorpe, had been a very liberal and progressive thinker and would have talked him round. This one – what was his name? – did not have an ounce of imagination or progressive thinking in him and did as he was told. He came to my classroom and told me to delete this book from my list. When I refused, he ordered me to do so with the predictable result that the next morning I handed in my letter of resignation.

I had left a small loophole. I wrote that I was not prepared to change my own list, but that I would, if needs be, remove it altogether or let the head of the department make up a list of his own to put up. Mr Crellin wouldn't hear of my resignation, suggested I remove the list and told me he'd have a word with the unmemorable head of English. No other list ever appeared. To give Crellin his due, when I was leaving, he asked: "Don't you want a testimonial?" I was surprised, since relations between us had been frosty since that incident, but not only had he written a glowing testimonial, describing me euphemistically as 'forthright', he also conceded to me as we said our farewells that *Saturday Night and Sunday Morning* was literature.

At the end of three years in Letchworth, Ernest was appointed professor at Aston University in Birmingham. We decided that, since our semi-detached life had gone very well during this time, we might as well live together permanently again.

Initially, Ernest took his mother with him to look for a suitable house. They went several times. Why did I not object? Was I still conditioned to playing second fiddle to his mummy? They came to no definite decision, but eventually, when I went with Ernest and time began to run out, he decided on the house I disliked the most: it was detached, with a large garden and practically impossible to run without help. To make matters worse, it was far from easy public access to anywhere in the city, which for me meant a great inconvenience. The residents of the street were wealthy, with all of the women being house-wives, whereas we both had to work full time to be able to afford it.

I had started looking for a post in Birmingham, and quite early on read about a new comprehensive school being built in a deprived area. I set my heart on this school and despite other adverts, waited until the official advert for Balsall Heath Comprehensive School appeared. My initial impression was negative: I received a handwritten postcard by the future headmistress, which arrived with the second post – hard to imagine now, but there were two deliveries a day – on a Friday, to invite me for an interview on the following Monday morning.

This meant I couldn't make any arrangement with my existing school. There was also a spelling mistake in the card. Despite this, I came to the half finished building in Birmingham on a cold and rainy Monday morning. The headmistress, Miss Hanks, led the various candidates through numerous corridors and half built classrooms, after which we left the building and all re-assembled at the Department of Education in the city.

We were being interviewed individually, with the rest of the candidates waiting outside the room. As it happened, I was sitting next to a young woman who had applied for the same post as I had done, teacher of English scale 1.

When my turn came, Miss Hanks offered me a scale 1 post as house-mistress, for which I hadn't applied.

"But I applied for a post as a teacher of English," I remonstrated. Miss Hanks simply ignored this and the interview went so badly that one of the city's inspectors, sitting in during the interviews, interrupted to tell me, "Never mind, Mrs Braun, there are plenty of other scale 1 posts for English teachers in Birmingham." Miss Hanks sat there stone-faced. At the end, I was told that I would be informed by post.

On the way home, I half wished that I wouldn't be offered the job and wouldn't have to make a decision, but within two days a letter arrived offering me the scale 1 house-mistress post. After hesitating at some length, I decided: "I'm not going to have much to do with the headmistress and I really want to teach the pupils at this school." And so I accepted.

Big mistake!

Balsall Heath School and its Headmistress, Miss Hanks or "Hanky Panky" in common parlance, proved worse than expected. She was constantly interfering, to the point of frequently entering the staff room unannounced, not to mention classrooms during lessons, usually with some trifling remark. I don't remember many staff meetings. She didn't do discussions. Instead, every time a problem came up, whether it concerned books, equipment, difficult pupils, financing or any other matter, we would receive a memo. Many of these didn't actually address the issues, but for her the matter was closed. There was a deluge of memos floating around the school. Still, I enjoyed most of my teaching time and made friends with other teachers.

One of them was the young woman, Patsy, who had applied for the same job as me. She was going through a difficult divorce and was rather flirtatious with most of the male staff. They in turn avoided her, despite her attractiveness: in particular the committed and married ones sensed danger.

One day in April, I took Patsy home after work, and as soon as Ernest clapped eyes on her the sparks were flying. It wasn't long before he returned later and later in the evenings, claiming work hold-ups.

"You know what it's like," he would say, semi-bashfully.

He never responded to my increasingly sarcastic

"Yes, I do know what it's like!"

During this time, we also received Manfred's modest inheritance, which had been contested by his young companion. Part of the money went on some decent furniture, but Ernest, by that time deeply in love with Patsy, suggested we offer her some money and it was best offered by him.

We still celebrated my mother in law's 70th birthday, as we were located very centrally, with family members coming from as far as Kent and Scotland. We had a very enjoyable lunch, which stretched with some of our guests till after tea and into the evening.

When the last guest had left, I sat down exhausted.

"I'm going to take the dog for a walk," announced Ernest,

"What, now?" Outside it was pouring.

"Yes, it's because..."

"I don't want to know, just go!" I shouted.

I cleared up and went to bed, but I couldn't sleep.

At about 11pm Smadar came into the bedroom: "Where's dad?"

"He's taken the dog for a walk."

"In this rain?" she asked, and after a short pause, "it's like Dundee again, isn't it?"

We had never told the girls about the reason for our split in Dundee. We said only that we were not getting on very well, but she had obviously gleaned the truth. After a short while, I stopped trying to make excuses and assented. Smadar must have already had some sneaking doubts about his frequent absences.

The next day I faced Ernest and he readily conceded: he loved Patsy and was very seriously involved with her.

My immediate reaction was, "I'm not going through this again. This time it's divorce."

He, of course, didn't believe it.

I lost count of the number of times I almost weakened, given the incessant pressure I was subjected to from him, his mother and his family, but didn't let myself, thanks in no small part to Sonia, a Swedish colleague and friend of mine who quashed my doubts again and again. What I had told her about the whole affair probably made her see much more clearly that for me to stay with Ernest would be insane. Fundamentally, I had lost trust in and respect for him.

Had I not gone through with this, how would I be able to hold my head up, especially since Ernest's strongest argument against divorce was that it would be a 'financial catastrophe'?

Meanwhile, much to the fury of Miss Hanks, I applied for a post as teacher of English and librarian scale 1 at Queensbridge School, a Comprehensive School nearby. I didn't want to be around Balsall Heath when the whole divorce saga was going to explode. Neither had the post as house-mistress given me much joy.

Chapter Twenty-seven

Queensbridge, my new school, was a pleasant experience, but even there the forthcoming divorce hung over me and my depression did not lift. At least I managed to introduce numerous books by African-Caribbean, African and Asian writers, reflecting the various backgrounds of the school's pupils. The popularity of this was noticeable when quite often pupils would push certain books to the back of the shelves so nobody could get at them first.

Ernest moved out sometime in late autumn of that year, but it wasn't until January of 1970 that the decree absolute came through. It seemed an eternity. The divorce was uncontested and Ernest undertook to pay for the girls as long as they were in full time education and for me offered the princely sum of £38 per month, unless I remarried. When I came out of the courthouse, I removed my wedding ring and exchanged it for my mother's black onyx and diamond ring, which I wear constantly to this day.

The next seven years were a nightmare, with me spiralling to practically rock bottom – one contributing factor was no doubt my new school in Birmingham after I had completed three years at Queensbridge. Once Smadar completed her

A-levels, I considered applying to a school in London, where I had always longed to live. I applied as deputy head of department at a school in Lambeth, South London, which I was very keen on. The atmosphere was very friendly and warm, the headmistress, governors – one of them Caribbean – and I, sat round a table and the interview seemed truly informal and went really well.

I was surprised and disappointed when at the end the headmistress said: "Well, we need to interview some other candidates," (I hadn't seen any), "but we'll let you know."

On my way out there was a woman sitting – I didn't associate her with any type of candidate.

On my way back to the tube, a car pulled up beside me. It was one of the governors.

"We really all wanted to have you," she explained, "but one of the teachers already at the school on scale 2 had also applied – had we appointed you over her head, it would have created tensions and bad blood. But we also have a geography post open at scale 3, would you consider applying for that?"

Never having taught geography, I had to decline her offer. Instead, I decided to apply as deputy head of department/librarian in Birmingham.

The first school I applied to was Four Dwellings Comprehensive School in Quinton. It was being newly amalgamated into a large comprehensive school from what had been an old fashioned girls' school and what was seen as a rough boys' school, with a new headmaster and various other changes. The interview didn't go too well. At the time, my own judgement was probably clouded, it was only 1971 and I was still in emotional turmoil.

Although I wouldn't credit Mr Richardson, the head, with my eventual complete breakdown, he certainly speeded things along. I managed to blot my book completely in the first week. On my list of items for the library was shelving and six armchairs amongst other things, but the latter did not appear. When I asked the men who were delivering and putting up the shelving, they shrugged, "You'll have to ask the headmaster about that, we did deliver them."

I went quite innocently to the head's office and there they were: six spanking new armchairs. "Are these the new library chairs?" I enquired.

"They will only get damaged or be vandalised in the library," came his answer.

"But I wasn't even informed!" I objected.

"Well, you are being informed now," said Richardson and showed me the door.

Outside I encountered a colleague who had been made responsible for all the school's stock.

"We can't have the library chairs because Mr Richardson wants them. Can we have his old ones instead?" I asked quite loudly.

The following day the deputy head, a yes-man if ever there was one, entered my classroom in a rage.

"Mr Richardson can do exactly as he wants in his school, he does not have to give an account to anyone!" he fumed at me and disappeared before I had time to utter a word.

But in many ways my fate was sealed.

Richardson was a particularly vindictive person. He reminded me of nothing so much as Captain Phillip Queeg from the *Caine Mutiny*: he mostly hid himself in his office and was remote and inaccessible. In staff meetings, he spoke almost inaudibly, never lifting his eyes and perpetually rolling a small eraser between finger and thumb. He also refused to see reality as it was. On one occasion there was a fight between a black and a white lad in the school ground, with a large mob surrounding them, shouting "we hate wogs!"

Richardson's response to enquiries from the local press was: "Racial harmony in the school is supreme."

By that time I had long become aware of prejudice and racism against Caribbean people, Africans and Asians and found myself completely unable to overlook any such incident. As a result, I was on very good terms with my non-European pupils, whereas some of the English ones occasionally commented, "Well, you're Jewish."

Explaining my total lack of religion would have been too complicated, so I let it slip.

Various members of staff, especially those from the old girls' school, were also blatantly racist. "Let's face it, they lower the tone," was one typical comment. This in itself made me very uncomfortable in the school, quite apart from my ever-downward spiralling state of mind.

By the mid seventies I felt desperate. The feeling of my utter worthlessness grew and I started drinking heavily at bedtime. Suicide seemed more and more like the only option.

Not long after I took up my post at Four Dwellings, we moved to a particularly pleasant and well-designed semi detached house, nearer to Four Dwellings School. Smadar was going to Colombia for a year to do research for her Ph.D. and shortly before her departure, married Tim, a pleasant and quiet co-student. To live as partners in Colombia still seemed unacceptable, but the spark between them was lacking. They seemed like a long-married couple. I relegated such doubts to the background. Who was I, half gin-soaked most of the time, to make a reasonable judgment? And how many couples were there who had never experienced this initial thrill?

It was not very long though, before Smadar met and fell in love with a young Colombian, Gonzalo Parra. Their love was mutual and a painful split from Tim followed. Eventually Gonzalo followed her to England. They married some time after this.

In a letter from Smadar dating from that time, she asked how and why I felt so negative about myself and my work. "But mummy," she wrote, "you are a good teacher. You could easily move to a different school."

I was convinced I would never find another job, not least owing to Richardson's frequent allusions to this fact. I saw no way out, became more suicidal with a strong urge to end it all. I was only looking for a way to make it look like an accident.

Luckily, before I could do anything I had a complete breakdown and ended up in the mental ward of Queen Elizabeth Hospital in Birmingham. It was a lifeline. My relief that I was not to blame for everything that had happened and in particular, my shame and guilt towards Smadar and even more so Yael, who was at that time still a student at Lancaster University, was palpable. Although the psychiatrist to whom I was assigned was not particularly good, the mere fact of my respite was of immense importance. Within a couple of weeks, hope and my will to live returned. After some six weeks, I was discharged.

A second lease of life had opened up, one that I held on to, despite initial difficulties. At school, Richardson decided that the only work I could undertake was part-time teaching. He used to come to my class, bend over me and say: "You'll never be able to hold down a full-time job."

This time I involved my union. Richardson appeared in my classroom stamping his foot.

"How dare you involve your union after all this?" he demanded.

He even designed a letter to the Department of Education saying that I had admitted myself into hospital and he tried to blame me regarding his repeated phone-calls to my psychiatrist, who unsurprisingly refused to discuss my case with him. The new deputy head, a very different and thoughtful person, showed me the letter and asked whether I wanted to cancel my involvement with my union. He also revealed that he was surprised since Richardson himself had had mental health issues.

"Let him," I shrugged.

I heard no further about the letter.

But I decided that I need not stay at the school in which I had been so unhappy. I had also become increasingly aware of the prevalent racism at the time. This had influenced me sufficiently to look for a post involving multiracial/multicultural students. The best opportunity seemed to be the Steward Centre for New Immigrants, designed to teach English as well as all other subjects in English for newcomers aged eleven upwards. They left when any of them was fluent enough to enter secondary education, a college or a job. It meant accepting a scale 2 post, but I decided that this was of minor importance.

My application was accepted. According to Richardson, I would never be able to teach full time and the best I could hope for was teaching immigrants.

Steward Centre was liberal, congenial and flexible. We were at liberty to teach our pupils in whatever method we felt was effective. I soon made friends with many of my pupils who came from all over the world, although mainly from the Indian sub-continent. I learnt so much about their various countries, traditions and customs that I often felt I learnt as much from them as they did from me.

There were also some hilarious instances such as the time when they kept trying to explain Plag-plying (flag-flying) over India, meaning independence. Even better was the event when Indira Gandhi, trying to be re-elected, travelled to various countries with Indian/Punjabi communities.

"Mrs Gandhi speaking at Odeon Cinema tomorrow night," they told me one Friday, "You go?"

"No," I replied, "I don't like her very much."

This was the signal for a deluge of derogative comments: "She stupid woman! She no good woman."

"She isn't stupid, but she isn't very nice," was my lame response.

The following Monday, my students couldn't wait to ask me, "You go to Odeon?"

"No. Did you?"

"Yes!" They proudly answered.

"But you said you didn't like her?"

"We go to throw the eggs!" came the proud reply.

And then there were my own mistakes, a litany of 'don'ts' for teachers. Just a couple of examples: in Balsall Heath School I once collected common mistakes pupils had made when writing compositions and put them on the board, asking them how they would correct them. One example was "There's some birds in the trees." The correction that most pupils wrote was: "There isn't no birds in the trees."

Later on at Steward Centre, when I introduced comparatives, I asked three girls of different heights to come to the front and the rest of the class had to compare, "Surinder is taller than", "X is shorter than", "Y is the shortest." Then I had the idea of comparing hair lengths and asked the girls to turn round.

Before I could say anything, one of the boys said, "Kulvinder has the biggest bottom." Kulvinder stomped off furiously and that was the end of my bright idea.

It was an invitation from some of my Hindu pupils to come with them to the last night of the Diwali celebrations at their temple that sparked an idea: I was already learning so much about my pupils' countries, traditions and customs, why not dance?

My old love of Dance awoke and I volunteered to organise an end of term ceremony, involving mainly Dance. There was a simple opening, performed by some 16 girls, after which each group/nationality showed something of their country: a dance, a song, a poem and more. At the end of this bi-annual celebration everybody, pupils as well as teachers, would participate in a simple round dance, usually of Balkan origin.

By that time I had joined a folk dance group myself, as well as a contemporary dance one. In the contemporary group we performed Mussorgsky's *Night on the Bare Mountain.*

Colour prejudice was still so prevalent that I was repeatedly asked whether I didn't want to be one of the angels. The devils by and large were of Caribbean origin. I insisted on being a devil. Quite apart from anything else, the angels' part was plain boring, though I didn't say so aloud. At opening night, we were almost too successful. I was crouching alone on stage and began snaking my way upwards as the music started.

"I want my mummy!" A little boy, whose mother was one of the angels, started screaming. I all but stopped mid-movement to call out, "It's only pretend."

The weekly folk dance group was very enjoyable. I started wondering, though, why we did not rope in the many communities in Birmingham. I tried to sell my idea to numerous institutions and NGOs, with the repeated response: "Very good idea, how are you going to organise it?"

The trouble was I didn't really want to organise anything, I was just there for the dancing. It took nearly a year before it dawned on me that, unless I undertook the organising, nothing would come of it. Eventually, I recruited another couple of enthusiasts, one of them Rashida Noor Mohammed from Kenya, who worked for the Council for Racial Equality and was completely secular. She was far more knowledgeable in matters not only of approaching communities, but almost more importantly, of obtaining funding. We received a grant from the Rowntree Foundation. Rashida became a staunch ally and friend of mine.

I also managed to rope in the Overseas Students' Association, which meant that even more communities got involved and that we had permission to use their Martin Luther King Hall at Aston University on a monthly basis, including their tea and coffee making facilities.

The following three years were probably some of the most productive ones of my life. I thought nothing of approaching strangers at bus stops or in supermarkets with an invitation to join us, and most of the time it worked. We managed to involve groups of Palestinians, Kurds, Bulgarians, Gujaratis, Bangladeshis, Greeks, Turks, Yemenis, West, North and South Africans, Poles and many more. By that time, I was most reluctant to invite Israelis, but the manager of the hall, a clergyman, insisted that I could not exclude them. But I cheated a little: instead of approaching any Israelis, I got some of the weekly folk-dance group I attended to come and teach a couple of Israeli dances.

And so we started and soon became widely known. We had to prepare a programme for the whole academic year in advance, which resulted in one visitor looking at it and asking:

"Do you specialise in dances of the underdog?" What a compliment!

Through these dances we could also trace the trails of the slave trade. One striking example was by Colombian versus West African songs and dances that traced the slave trade very clearly.

Whole families came to the monthly events, soon to become widely popular. We always started with repetition of the dances we had learnt the previous time, after which the group whose turn it was would teach us some of their dances. A lengthy break followed, during which each group would sell us some of their specialities at cost price. After this we would practise the newly learned dances once more before the session came to an end.

We finally decided on a rather clumsy name, The Birmingham Minority Folk-Dance Group. Meanwhile, I parted from my previous folk-dance group on a sour note. I had enthusiastically described to our tutor the wide possibilities open to us if we asked the people from the Birmingham Minorities Folk-Dance Group to join us, but her response shocked me:

"We don't want to be swamped by Asians."

To my reply, "But you call yourself international?" she countered, "European, Hanna, European."

Once it sank in that she was quite serious, I wrote her an angry letter saying, "As I am myself of Jewish origin, I regard myself as Semitic and thus Asian. In future I shall not attend your classes."

Her response was even more bizarre: she just loved Jews and some of her best friends etc. I didn't reply and no longer went, but quite a few people from her class started attending ours as well. When I mentioned the whole affair to Rashida, she wasn't at all surprised. She had noted the woman's racism the first time she met her. I still had a lot to learn.

Some of us, particularly Rashida and I, started being invited to various colleges to lead workshops. As a result, we gained more members.

In the second year, I was asked to participate in the 'One World Week' in Birmingham. One World Week? What about all the other weeks? Anyway, we had to find a suitable venue, as the Martin Luther King Hall was far too small. Someone suggested the Cooperative Hall that was located above the store. All went well until we came to the catering part: "Oh no, we can't have foreign food! It's because of the smell."

"You mean like over-boiled cabbage?" I snapped.

It looked as if our idea was doomed from the start, but rescue appeared in the shape of the vicar of Saint Martin's Church. St Martin's had a large hall incorporating a stage and the various food smells did not disturb the religious authorities in the least.

And so we could proceed. We asked each group to bring food in large quantities. We also asked them to give us their recipes, which our deputy head at the Steward Centre edited and printed out in small booklets. These were on sale and went very quickly. As to drinks, we got hold of the services of a mobile bar. They brought all their drinks and equipment and operated independently from us.

We eventually came up with two events on the day. In the afternoon, a workshop, a kind of preparation for the evening's event. The evening was to be a huge party with food, drink and some of our dances performed on stage. It wasn't all smooth sailing. Who would perform and when caused some ruffling of feathers.

Everyone was to come in their national costumes for the evening party. When one of the English members asked me what they should wear, my not very kind advice was, "Just paint yourself in woad." We had it all worked out except for ticket sales. They went so badly, that in the week leading up to the event Barry, our treasurer, phoned all the groups and asked them to make only half the quantities of food.

On the day itself, after a sluggish start, more people than we had expected turned up, but the evening took us completely by surprise. Most people had decided to buy their tickets at the door. After initial delight, we panicked as the hall was getting too packed, with not enough food to go round. I asked those at the door to stop selling tickets and only let in ticket holders, while Barry rushed to the kitchen and with a large knife cut every portion in half.

Some time during the evening, Smadar and Gonzalo appeared. They had spent the day in Leeds and hadn't expected to make it. They were refused entry. All their pleas fell on deaf ears, only ticket holders were let in. It was only when Smadar exclaimed, "But she's my mother!" that the doorman relented, provided that they promised faithfully not to eat anything. The evening ended with the Punjabi Bhangra dancers, who ended up jumping from the stage and getting us all to dance with them. The whole place was teeming with dancers! What an unforgettable event for me. I still feel a warm glow in retrospect.

PART THREE
1982–1989

SEMI-RETIREMENT AND INTENSIVE POLITICAL ACTIVITY

Chapter Twenty-eight

For many years I had been an anti-apartheid activist, yet completely failed to make the connection between apartheid and the Israeli occupation.

I was increasingly sceptical of the Zionist idea, but I was stumbling, with only a few books to help me along. It wasn't until I met some Palestinian students that I started to understand their views far more clearly.

My newfound friends, with endless patience, pointed me in the direction of a wealth of literature, which in itself came as a great surprise to me. Modern Arabic literature, how come I had never heard of it?

But perhaps the greatest novelty was these young Palestinians themselves. They were so much like us when we had been their age, with their aspirations, humour and friendships. And they showed endless forbearance with me and with what must have been my often clumsy and ignorant questions.

I particularly remember Moussa Howari, from a wealthy Christian family in Jerusalem, who was the chair of the Palestinian Students' Association. I took him to Steward Centre on one occasion to talk and answer questions on Palestine, little suspecting that there would come a time in my life when I would perform the same task very frequently.

Moussa was always courteous and calm, with a sharp sense of humour, although there was one occasion that is fixed firmly in my mind, when his depth of bitterness and anger erupted.

We were sitting in his room, talking about racism. He accused Israelis of blatant racism. When I protested that he shouldn't generalise, he suddenly burst out with his own experience: he had become friendly with a fellow student (Moussa had completed his first year at the Hebrew University in Jerusalem). The girl was from Iraq, spoke fluent Arabic and was steeped in the traditions and customs of the Arab world.

Moussa and the girl started going out together, but she broke it off after a short while.

"Why? She wasn't even religious. But I'm Arab and so I'm unacceptable as an equal in my own country! She was ashamed of me."

I stood by mutely. I had never before truly taken in how Palestinians felt about the occupation of their homeland.

The only thing I could do was to make sure that I always included Palestinians in various events, such as asking round ten or so people for dinner, which always included some Middle Eastern food. I also came to support them at various events at the University in which they participated.

On one occasion, the Palestinian students invited me to a talk given by Yossef Abilea, director of the Music Conservatory in Haifa and a long-term pacifist, whom I had known many years ago, when I was a schoolgirl. He had just returned from a tour in the USA, a frail old man, who, together with his wife, was still striving for justice and equality for all.

Another student who became a friend was Sami Boustami. His uncle, Bassam Shaka'a, was the then mayor of Nablus and very outspoken about the Israeli occupation. He had been summoned to the office of Ezer Weitzman, Israel's president at the time, for a confidential meeting, during which Weitzman threatened him with liquidation if he continued his policies of non-compliance. Mr Shaka'a made some inflammatory remarks in Weitzman's presence and was initially jailed, with the Israeli government ordering him to be deported.

The supreme court of Israel overturned the decision (unthinkable nowadays!) and Shaka'a returned to a triumphant welcome in Nablus. Not only did he refuse to comply, he publicised the confidential meeting widely with foreseeable results: a terrorist group, with the help of the Israeli Secret Services, booby-trapped the mayor's car. Barely escaping with his life, he had to have both legs amputated.

Sami never spoke about it and I only learned about this from another student. When he was leaving for the States, he came with another friend to say goodbye to me. Sami showed a true generosity of spirit and never lumped all Jews or Israelis together.

He, like many of my Palestinian friends, continued their education in the US after Margaret Thatcher had become Prime Minister and grants to overseas students were cut.

Once I started reading about the truth of what Zionism was aiming at: to get rid of all the local population and make the country a completely Jewish state, I began to devour books by Palestinian writers, in particular Edward Sa'id, Rosemary Sayigh and others as well as some of the right wing Zionists, such as Jabotinsky, an early Zionist who advocated an "Iron wall" quite openly. It became painfully clear that the Right, including the extremists, and the Left didn't differ in ideology, their differences were purely those of tactics and strategy.

This led me increasingly away from Zionism and what it stands for: a colonial, racist settler state. But it took the invasion of Lebanon in 1982, engineered by Ariel Sharon, to turn me from a non-Zionist to an anti-Zionist. At a large demonstration in London, I met a number of Israelis/Jews who took the same stand. I was not alone!

Shortly after the demo in London, I had an idea.

Birmingham Museum and Art Gallery had a mobile educational section with artefacts from the Indian subcontinent and from various African countries. I thought it would be great to display Palestinian artefacts. I approached the gallery and they were happy to receive such a mobile exhibition, provided I organised it.

What now? I hadn't really thought this through. I turned to Leila Mantoura, a good Palestinian friend living in London, and she suggested I contact Sheilagh Weir, who at the time worked at the Museum of Mankind in London.

I went to see Sheilagh at her flat and she suggested I contact a Palestinian friend of hers, the painter and artist Vera Tamari, who was spending a sabbatical year in Oxford.

I did so and in due course two suitcases arrived with the most delightful artefacts: mother of pearl handicraft and jewellery from Bethlehem, olive wood statuettes, beautifully embroidered dresses and, most of all, Palestinian children's own paintings and drawings. Smadar helped me lug the suitcases to the Museum. I phoned Vera to thank her. But, when I suggested she come for just one occasion to join our Palestinian dancers, she put down her foot very firmly.

At the end of the time I was later to spend in Zimbabwe, I phoned the gallery in Birmingham to find out the fate of the exhibition.

"Sorry, but you can't have it at the moment. It's on loan".

What a great surprise! Some years later a former colleague told me the exhibition was still alive and kicking. Evidently, this was one of the exceptions that the Board of Jewish Deputies hadn't yet discovered and managed to stifle.

Chapter Twenty-nine

Not long after Zimbabwe's independence, in 1981, my first grandson, Camilo, was born and I had to decide what I wanted him to call me once he started speaking. Neither the English Nana, nor Granny appealed and I had the bright idea of settling on Imma (mummy in Hebrew and the name I had used for my own mother). It was neither bright, nor unique, as once Camilo started school, all the Asian kids assumed he was my son, since Umma is used in their languages for Mother and vowels, in Semitic languages at any rate, play a slightly minor role and are often almost interchangeable.

"Your mum is waiting by the gate," they would tell Camilo, and when he said that I was his grandmother, not his mum, they'd respond with, "Then why do you call her mum?"

Gonzalo's mother, who had become a reborn Christian, kept phoning from the States where she had moved to, pleading for Gonzalo to have the baby baptised. On one occasion, when both he and Smadar complained that she had phoned yet again, I said, "When she next phones, tell her that if he's baptised I also want him circumcised."

Gonzalo looked quite worried, "Do you want him circumcised?" he asked.

"I couldn't care less, but just tell her."

It worked like magic. Two more grandsons followed and the subject was never mentioned again.

In early 1982, a notice appeared on the staff-room notice board offering all teachers aged 52 and over seven years' enhanced pension, provided they took early retirement. I wasn't in the least interested. I didn't feel like retiring. But when the rumour went around that at the end of the year all teachers aged 55 and over would be forcibly retired without any pension enhancement, I became anxious. I had neither lived nor worked sufficient years to receive a full pension as it was.

Meanwhile, the war in Zimbabwe continued with secret aid from British sources, despite the official embargo. Ian Smith broke the agreement to let Africans vote at least in some numbers. There had been a short-lived interim Republic of Zimbabwe–Rhodesia, which had not achieved any significant change for the large majority of the African population. Most of my friends as well as I were part of the anti-apartheid movement and thus agreed with the Zimbabweans, who were fighting a war for independence. To many in the British government, let alone the whites in Rhodesia, they were simply terrorists.

It was only when the Zimbabweans started to gain the upper hand that the British hastily convened a peace conference at Lancaster House in London, to try and bring about a peaceful solution. ZANU (headed by Robert Mugabe) and ZAPU (headed by Joshua Nkomo) made some concessions, but basically there were to be free elections for the first time.

Smith, who had ruled the roost for many years, put up as many obstacles as possible. On the voting papers, no symbols or characters were to be allowed, the reason being that many rural people were illiterate and so were not able to put their crosses in the correct place, but the bush post was faster. When Election Day came, everyone had been informed who the parties were. Mugabe won a landslide victory. We had been sitting glued to the TV that night and the elation and celebrations were great.

And so when I came across an advertisement by the new Government of Zimbabwe in the Education Guardian, which read, "Help us build up our Secondary Education" I knew exactly what I wanted to do. Prior to independence, only 8% of African children were allowed secondary education in state schools.

I phoned Smadar excitedly.

"They are looking for secondary school teachers in Zimbabwe!"

"Don't be silly, mummy, they'll never take you. You are much too old."

I waited for a week, but when the same advert appeared the following Tuesday, I wrote to ask for an application form. Not long after this, I was invited to the Zimbabwean Embassy in London where my interviewer, a white ex-Rhodesian, was somewhat surprised. Most applications had come from young teachers. I was at the other end of the spectrum: With both my daughters working, I was free to go. Mr Trevellyan accepted me there and then.

A friend of a friend warned me not to go to what had been 'A' schools: they had been exclusively white schools and he warned me:

"You wouldn't last more than a term in such a school, Hanna!" He remembered one particular township called

Highfield and I repeatedly wrote in my correspondence that I would like to be placed at Highfield High School.

Meanwhile, my second grandson, Daniel, put a spanner in the works. I was initially supposed to start in September, but with one toddler and one newborn, with just a year between them, Smadar soon became exhausted. She accepted my offer to postpone my departure until Christmas with great relief.

I wrote to the Ministry of Education in Zimbabwe and explained that I had to postpone my arrival in Zimbabwe till just after Christmas. It didn't seem a particularly awkward request, since the school year in Zimbabwe starts at the beginning of January.

When the time approached, no flight tickets, nor for that matter any communication, appeared despite my increasingly anxious letters. I became seriously worried and eventually resorted to writing a strongly worded letter to the Zimbabwean Ministry of Education with a cc to the Guardian. I didn't send the cc, but it made all the difference. Very soon after this, my ticket arrived. I was to travel overnight on Friday by Air Zimbabwe and would be met by an official on Saturday morning.

My departure was gut-wrenching. As usual, I had jumped in before thinking the whole thing through. A friend of mine, Donna Williams, drove me to Heathrow for my flight to Harare. I swallowed my tears and boarded the plane.

The next morning, there was nobody from the ministry to tell me where to go. I knew that we were supposed to stay in a hotel for three weeks without payment, after which we would have to fend for ourselves. I chatted to a Zimbabwean who was also waiting and asked him where the government usually put up new ex-pats.

"Oh," he said, "That'll be the Meikle's Hotel, I can drive you there if you like."

I took up his offer gratefully and we drove to what was a luxury hotel. As soon as we arrived, I knew I was in the wrong place. By now it was Saturday evening.

Fortunately, I had the Birmingham friend's telephone number of his friend in Harare, Joshua Nyoka. I phoned him and he arrived quite soon afterwards and insisted I spend the weekend at his and his wife's house. Both Joshua and his wife Carmel, who was Jamaican by origin, made me most welcome.

At the time, there was a whole group of Jamaican women who had met and married Zimbabweans who had to flee their country during the war. Some of them contributed greatly to their new surroundings. One of them became the new director of the Harare Museum and Art Gallery. During her time, the art gallery changed completely from a collection of fairly boring, white, middle class paintings, to highly imaginative works by Zimbabwean as well as other artists from the southern hemisphere.

Carmel was less fortunate: her husband Joshua was quite stupid and had no sensitivity at all. In the second year, she went for a month's visit to England and when she visited me after her return, it was clear that she was heading for a complete breakdown.

On Monday morning, Joshua took me to the Ministry of Education. My interviewer was the same man I had spoken to in London. To my dismay, I had been placed in Mabelreign High School for Girls with free accommodation. I had an increasingly acrimonious conversation with Mr Trevellyan.

Eventually, shaking with rage, he asked, "And why do you only want to teach black children?"

"I wasn't thinking so much of colour, but rather of economic status. I believe Highfield needs experienced teachers more than Mabelreign."

He stomped off in a fury to find a car. All this had been in the presence of an African secretary. While I was waiting, I apologised to her but she just laughed and shrugged it off. When Mr Trevellyan returned, he drove me to Highfield High School, some 20 minutes' drive, without saying a word. Most uncomfortable, but worse was to come: At the school, the headmaster at that time was still white and Trevellyan's conversation with him made me want to creep under a table.

"Mrs Braun does not *wish* to teach at Mabelreign School. She *prefers* Highfield High School."

Eventually, he left without giving me any idea of how to get back to Harare again.

I was shown to my classroom, which, like the whole building, was of a very basic structure: cement floors and walls, a zinc roof from which naked bulbs hung (and quite often were nicked).

During the first two months, my salary cheque was still being sent to Mabelreign High School. When I saw the place, it seemed absolutely luxurious compared to Highfield: parquet flooring, a tennis court, a swimming pool and more. But the comments from the teachers were so racist that I was very glad that I hadn't gone there.

At Highfield the number of my pupils was overwhelming. Between 45 and 50 students attended one of two shifts. There was the morning shift from 7am to 12.30pm, the afternoon one, from 1pm to 6.30pm. On top of this, there were adult literacy classes from seven till nine.

The school was literally bursting at the seams! The pupils were also incredibly motivated: this was the first time all African pupils had full rights to secondary education, unlike the measly 8% prior to independence.

During the second week, I needed to transfer some books and papers from the storeroom and asked one of the boys, Tzingwayi, to come with me and help. Tzingwayi asked his twin brother to come, calling him loudly 'Nigger!'

Or so I thought.

"That's a horrible word," I told him, "You should never use that word."

Tzingwayi looked bemused.

"What word?" he asked.

"You said 'nigger'!" I accused him.

"I said Nyika, that's his name."

It was my turn to apologise.

Initially, the names of my pupils posed a puzzle because of their length. It was very common to have surnames of five or more syllables. Where do you put the stress on Matanyatumba, MbuyaNehanda or Monomatapa? I soon cottoned on, though, that the stress is always on the penultimate syllable, as it is in many African languages. As to first names, they could be very amusing at times: I had one pupil called Doesn't Matter as well as another named It Matters Not. Then there was Last One (how could they be so certain?) and at times I seemed to have some of the characters from Snow White and the Seven Dwarves, such as Lucky, Smart (unfortunately he wasn't) and even Handsome.

Before the books arrived, I gave my pupils sheets of paper, explaining that I had never been to their country before and asked them to describe it to me. I had some very interesting descriptions, particularly about the beauty, the independence war, the apparently amazing fact that they had some white teachers now. One boy wrote: "Most people in Zimbabwe are black, a few are white and then there are some people I cannot mention." When I returned the compositions, I beckoned him to come to my desk and asked, "Who are those people you cannot mention?"

"Coloureds," he all but whispered.

"Coloureds?" I retorted. "But we are all coloured. Some of us are more coloured than others."

I lifted a sheet of paper.

"If you look like that you are dead," I said. The whole class stared at me. Was this woman mad? Completely ignorant?

I soon became enlightened about the resentment of Africans towards mixed race people. The latter often were employed in lowly positions as post office clerks or other administrative jobs. But with this came an important bonus: those who had regular employment received free healthcare prior to independence. The majority of Africans, who worked as casual labourers and were by and large the poorest sector, had to pay for healthcare if they could afford it: a big *if*.

This resentment had nothing racial about it. I came across several people in Highfield who were obviously of mixed race. One young woman used to grin broadly at me in the bus queue returning to town. Although her features were African, her colouring was a great deal lighter than mine.

Another cause of bewilderment was that in Shona, the common language spoken in Northern Zimbabwe and part of the Midlands, the letter L is not pronounced.

One morning after assembly – and how lustily the pupils sang! – one of the boys in my class was missing.

"Where's Musoni?" I asked. I had seen him go into assembly.

"He's praying," was the response.

"What, now?"

"He's praying for the schoor."

This sounded alarming. I looked around at the walls and the roof. (We had no ceiling). My pupils came to my rescue.

"He's praying footbar, Mrs Braun!

After this, I found it easier to understand a variety of words that I had failed to make sense of before.

Radio Zimbabwe regularly broadcast news and comments about Zionist Israel. Shortly after my arrival, I had met and made friends with two teachers from England, Joan and Dave Harries. On one occasion, while we were lying by the Olympic swimming pool in Harare, Dave asked me what I felt about these comments.

"They are absolutely right," I said.

Dave sat bolt upright.

"I had to come all the way to Zimbabwe to meet an anti-Zionist Israeli!"

I had to assure him that I was not unique, although I had to admit that there are not many of us.

Despite the nightmare of correcting up to fifty compositions, I enjoyed my time at Highfield greatly, making friends with staff and pupils alike.

184

During this period, I also contacted the PLO representative in Zimbabwe, Ali Halimeh, who had ambassador status there.

I invited him to many O- and A-level classes to talk about Israel and Palestine. Unfortunately, he wasn't a very good speaker. But at least I managed to hand him a list of books for the library in Harare, which had previously stocked only pro-Israel and very Zionist books.

In my third year of teaching, the Ministry of Education sent me to Allan Wilson High School for Boys. By that time, both staff and pupils were completely racially mixed and the atmosphere had changed totally, excepting a few dyed in the wool 'Rhodies' who still couldn't come to terms with racial equality.

Usually, my retorts to Rhodies anywhere were very sharp-tongued, but there was one memorable occasion when it was all I could do to stop myself from laughing out loud. I had gone to an elderly Italian hairdresser to have my hair cut.

"There's no future for us here any longer," he said sadly.

"Oh, why is that?" I asked.

"Well, you see, I have two sons. Before independence, whatever their school grades or attendance, they had a decent job guaranteed for life. But now," he sighed sadly, "It's all according to merit!"

With the sixth form, in which most of the white pupils still had their deep seated racial prejudices, I initiated a debating club quite deliberately made up of newcomers (black) and long-term pupils (white), so that they had to face each other and hear some much needed home truths. We also competed in a short play between the houses. (I had ended up being a house mistress again). The pupils had chosen the play within the play from *A Midsummer Night's Dream* and we hammed it up for all it was worth.

The boy playing Thisbe was particularly outstanding. It was a great success. The gym horse, with a white sheet over it and large letters proclaiming "Ninny's Tomb" served admirably. One of the boys was supposed to spread blood on the stage at the relevant time.

"Just spread some tomato ketchup," was my advice.

"I'll take the label off," he offered.

"No, enlarge it as much as possible so that the audience can plainly see the words 'Tomato Ketchup'," I said.

From then on, the boys cottoned on to the idea of ham acting and irony and enjoyed improvising by themselves. I particularly remember Thisbe holding up Pyramus' black arm and lamenting, "His hand, so lily white". And then there was the dead Pyramus himself, prone on Ninny's Tomb, who raised himself onto his elbows so swiftly that Thisbe, who had been lying across him, fell off and sat rubbing his bottom. "Now am I dead," he grinned cheerfully, "My soul is fled..."

One memorable test I had to pass was during our reading of Ngugi Wa Thiongo's *The River Between*, which includes a detailed description of circumcision.

That morning at the start of the lesson, a pupil from an Indian Muslim family asked me, "What is circumcision?"

"Well, you should know."

He mumbled something, but I could see all the pupils' faces looking at me expectantly. I decided to take the bull by the horns. Sitting on the desk, I gave a graphic description of the act of circumcision, by the end of which everybody had their noses in their books.

"Any more questions?" I asked.

"No! It's arright, Mrs Braun," was their response, except for one brave soul who asked about female circumcision.

"That's mutilation," I exclaimed. But when I started on the vagina and the labia, they'd had enough.

"Let's just carry on reading."

Zimbabwe is a county of outstanding beauty and I managed to see many of the beautiful and historic sites. In my third year, Yael, my youngest, came for a visit and together we saw some places suggesting a great past such as the Zimbabwe ruins and the wall paintings inside the Domboshawa Rocks.

During my three years I also visited Kenya and Malawi, the latter being possibly the most beautiful country I have ever seen, but from what I observed, one of the poorest. On the recommendation of friends, I went for a holiday to Lake Malawi in the 1984 Easter Holidays. The flight was the easy bit, although the airport at the time was just a strip of land with a hut serving as customs, passport control and, I hope, first aid station.

After this, I joined forces with a young woman, also from Zimbabwe, to find a recommended hostel in Lilongwe. Eventually, we gave up and stayed at a monastery, which also had some modestly priced rooms to let.

We were told the bus to the lake would be leaving at 7am and made sure to be at the bus station early.

What we hadn't anticipated was the length of the journey. It was just under eight hours and all on wooden benches. Once we arrived, we had to use the only phone in the village to contact the camp owner/manager and inform him of our arrival. (We omitted our sore behinds). He appeared in a van with three more people travelling to the lake, and drove us through what seemed to be a jungle. By then, it was much too dark to discern any road. The bumpy ride took another hour and a half to the camp.

"I only hope it's worth it," I commented to the young woman from Zimbabwe.

We were put up in a bungalow for that night and slept like logs. The next morning, we saw the beautiful clear water of the lake in front of us, with some Frangipani trees just outside the bungalow. Magical beauty!

The owner came to see us quite soon. He explained the different types of accommodation and their prices, from tents to dormitories to shared bungalows and to the real luxury, single bungalows. I opted for luxury. It meant one bed was removed, although the bungalow was still built for two, but with a separate entrance and shower/toilet. Only the porch was shared. The price, including three meals a day, was just under £5 per day. My companion decided to stay on her own outside the camp in a tent she had brought along.

The weather and swimming were wonderful. One day we decided to go by boat with the owner to a small island in the centre of the lake from which you could snorkel and observe numerous exotic fish.

It started to be a little windy as we left, but some of us had already chosen to swim back. My idea. From the shore, the distance looked quite short. At the tip of the island, about fifteen of us jumped off the boat and started swimming. All went well, but it had become quite choppy, with an overcast sky. After a while, I found myself completely alone. Not a soul in front of me, behind me, nor anywhere nearby. Even the boat had disappeared. I continued, but felt uncomfortable. I couldn't even lie on my back to have a rest, because of the waves. To my left, the mountains of Mozambique should signal that I was nearing the shore, but I swam and swam without seeing them. And where was everybody else?

Eventually, after what seemed ages, I glimpsed the mountains and knew I would be all right. It took quite a while still to reach the shore and when I did, two anxious young swimmers who had started off swimming alongside me but had then overtaken me, welcomed me with relief. I was the third one to swim all the way.

It turned out that, apart from us three, all the others had climbed back onto the boat at various stages, so the boat stayed behind to collect them. But I felt quite proud anyway: to achieve this feat at fifty-seven felt great when the other two were still in their twenties and early thirties respectively.

My guess had been that the distance was approximately two kilometres; only later did I find out that it was almost four. Had I known that, I wouldn't have dreamt of suggesting we swim ashore.

The camp had no electricity, so we all had paraffin lamps, and as to the meals, it rather depended on the catch of the day and on what was available in the village. Luckily, three meals of rice a day only happened once during my stay. In the evenings, we would often gather at the large communal bungalow, which was better lit and had a radio. Local people from the next village joined us frequently as well. Several times during an evening they would suddenly jump to their feet to stand up straight. It was the national anthem being played.

In Zimbabwe as well as in Malawi, friends, both African and European, would tease me, telling me I was born the wrong colour when I joined local dances. A great compliment to me. My love of Dance dated back to my youth. I had long ago determined that, if local people got up to dance anywhere, except northern Europe, where dances were performed almost exclusively in couples, I would be able to participate.

One day, a young man approached my bungalow. He had been told there was a former Israeli in the camp. When I assented, he explained he was travelling through Africa and he saw no reason not to visit South Africa. He was also a typical Israeli: whereas another holiday maker asked me whether it would be at all possible to stay overnight in my flat in Harare, the Israeli simply announced, "I'm going to stay with you when I come to Zimbabwe."

I wish I had said no. He turned out to be a fervent Zionist who wouldn't stop arguing. To make matters worse, he completely ate up any prepared meals I had made for the two of us before going to work. I was glad to see the back of him.

And then there was my personal life.

I made many friends, but in the first week in the hotel we were staying at, I met a young South Indian from a Christian family, who was at Harare University. The mutual attraction was immediate.

"*He is awfully young,*" I reasoned, but, as I already had found a flat into which I could move within the next three weeks, I reckoned a short fling would do no harm.

The three weeks extended to three years. We became very close and it was probably the best and longest affair of my life, despite the age difference.

In the third year, some tensions between ZANU and ZAPU became more marked in Zimbabwe, with ZANU members sometimes using their membership as a veiled threat. But, by and large, it was still a great and beautiful country. My contract came to an end in January 1986, but I postponed my departure until February.

Chapter Thirty

As I had taken early retirement, I was not eligible for my pension for almost another year. As before, I looked in the Guardian Educational for a post abroad and the most interesting one was a brand new university, Bilkent, just outside Ankara. I applied and was interviewed by one of the professors. I was accepted as a lecturer in the English department. This was a grandiose name. It was supposed to be an English-speaking university, but the students by and large spoke very little English and they formed the English Department. In reality, it was simply that of teaching basic English to non-English speakers. But then, many things in Turkey turned out to be not what they seemed, as I soon learned.

As in Zimbabwe, I was allowed one cubic metre crate to bring my belongings, quite apart from personal items. Unlike Zimbabwe however, the crate ended up in a depot outside Ankara. The head administrator sent me with a driver and a van to retrieve my crate. We were sent from one office to another and, to my disbelief, the driver never turned his back while we exited. He walked backwards, frequently bowing to his superiors. Were we still in the Ottoman era? Eventually, we arrived at the right place. The official (more bows) led us to the storeroom and I soon identified my crate. And then he demanded 300 Turkish lira to release it. For a moment I stood open mouthed, then laughed.

"In that case you can keep it, there's nothing of that much value in it," I said.

"Well then, 30 lira."

"I'm not paying that either, keep the crate."

In the end we settled for 3 lira, which at the time would have been a generous tip to a beggar.

The university was completely corrupt, despite the wonderful reputation it had. It was a private one and the students, or rather their parents, had to pay in dollars. Only the few who were on bursaries were truly intelligent and hard working. As for the others, we used to see them sporadically, mainly in the large hall, playing table tennis.

When the first term exams came in December, foreseeably, the bulk of the students failed, while those on bursaries got very high marks. We used to do the marking in pairs and were just finalising one of the bursary students' marks.

We were sitting in the canteen when we saw him.

"We have just finished marking your paper, would you like to know the score?" asked my colleague, Lisa. He seemed hesitant, maybe a bit scared and then nodded.

"You've received 86.7%."

As he turned to go, Lisa said, "Did you see the tears in his eyes?"

But when the results were published on the hall's notice board, lo and behold, everyone had passed quite well! We tried to complain, but were told it was too late to change anything.

What was particularly riling was the thought that all of the students, including those who couldn't form a single sentence in English to save their lives, would end up with the same type of degree. As it turned out, I was somewhat mistaken in this assumption. Years later when I taught some German at Coventry University, one of my students, a Turk with a sister at Bilkent, said that the rich and lazy students passed their exams and of course paid their fees for three years, only to be failed and excluded at the end of their third year of the four year course.

And that was only part of the Bilkent saga. The library was a complete mess since the American librarian wasn't really anything of the kind. She was just a friend of the owner and blissfully unaware of the Dewey system. Neither had she any idea of what kind of books to order.

Hierarchy was all-important. You didn't talk back to your superior, whatever they demanded. Everyone in the English Department was unhappy with the way things were run, but there was a big hurdle: If you broke your two-year contract, you had to repay one month's salary, the shipment of your crate and of course the return ticket. Quite a few colleagues had already left, either by not returning from holiday or by disappearing overnight.

As to me though, I was truly lucky in this respect. Just before I was to depart for my summer holiday, a letter was hand delivered on a Friday, long after office hours. It informed me that in September I would have to move to a smaller apartment.

"Very smart," I thought, "they now think I'll be unable to do anything about it until I return and by then it will be too late."

One of my colleagues, a friend married to a Turk, was still on campus. I wrote a furious letter, saying that I regarded the university in breach of contract and announcing that I would resign in October. This way I could be home for Christmas. My colleague, Soraya, was going to deliver the letter to the office on Monday.

Their breach of contract was really a welcome ruse. The original stated that I would be allocated flat number three in building number one for as long as I worked at the university. In reality, the flat was too large for me, but it served admirably to get me away from Bilkent.

Chapter Thirty-one

When I arrived for my holiday in Coventry in 1987, to where Smadar and her family had moved, Smadar, who was expecting again, felt that she was about to give birth. I was very keen about the date, the 28th of June, which had been my mother's birthday, but Nico, my youngest grandson, started life as he meant to go on: he almost appeared, then changed his mind and wasn't born until the following day.

Since my house was still occupied, I stayed with Smadar and her family until it was time to return to Turkey.

Upon my return to Bilkent, it turned out that neither the Head of the Department, nor that of the Administration had taken me seriously. I had asked not to be given a responsibility post again as I had no intention of staying the whole year, but had not been relieved of it.

Eventually I took a photocopy of my contract to the Rector of the University and showed him black on white that the university was in breach of it.

From then on, things changed rapidly. I was asked to teach English to a group of lecturers and it emerged that the English Speaking University was yet another nonsense. Meanwhile, I gave in my notice to leave on the 20th of December.

Not long after this, my bell rang one evening and there stood the vice principal, looking slightly embarrassed.

"Would you mind very much if you were to leave a month earlier? We would pay you an extra month's salary of course, as well as the payment of the crate and your return flight." He asked.

I barely restrained myself from shouting out "Yippee!" and instead consented quietly to his proposal.

Out of twenty lecturers in the department, I was the eighth to leave, but the first to do it openly. The idea that someone would stand up to authority, and a woman at that, set a precedent that they did not want leaked into the public domain.

And yet, how beautiful the country is, were it not for the people who were running it back then! Majestic mountains, the lovely Mediterranean which, at the time, was still practically free of tourists, the Black sea, Mount Ararat, Cappadocia and more. Istanbul deserves a chapter to itself, particularly the old part, which is actually in Europe, a tiny part of Istanbul separated from the mainland by the Bosporus. It is the most interesting part with its old streets, mosques and other antiquities. It still had the Middle-Eastern character, which Kamal Ata-Turk had striven so hard to rid Turkey of so as to make it into a European one: echoes of the idea of European superiority, familiar to me from Israel.

Yael came to visit me one Easter, but we only half enjoyed it, with the mosquito-like men who were almost impossible to shake off and the cold weather that particular year.

I returned home for good towards the end of November and again stayed with Smadar, but was able to return soon to my lovely home in Birmingham. I had agreed to look after my grandchildren during the week, but it soon emerged that this was not a practical solution. The train journey in the mornings to Coventry and in the evenings home left me no time or energy to do anything else, and so I decided to sell up and move to Coventry myself. Around that time, Yael had also moved to Coventry, after a stint in London, and had become self-employed.

I hadn't expected to sell my house as rapidly as I did. It never occurred to me that it would be quite so attractive to others. I had given it to the agents on a Monday and on Tuesday, when I came back from Coventry, there was a young man standing in front of my house. No sign had been put up as yet. He told me he had seen the details at the agent's and wondered when it would be possible to view the house.

"You can have a look now if you like," I said.

I showed him around and he kept saying, "It's nice, isn't it?" up to the point of me telling him that if he went on like that, I might decide not to sell.

At the end of his visit, we agreed that, since he had never bought a house as yet, he wanted to ask his Mother, who lived elsewhere, to come and have a look at it before making a final offer. We agreed that she would come on the following Saturday.

On Wednesday lunchtime, the estate agents phoned me in Coventry and said, "He has made an offer for the full price."

"But he was going to bring his Mother to look at it," I replied.

"He already has, he got her to come this morning."

It was the quickest house sale I have ever made.

Finding a house in Coventry proved a great deal more difficult. Nothing could really match my house in Birmingham, but eventually I settled into a pleasant house within walking distance of Smadar and Yael.

Now I had a great deal more time on my hands.

My main political involvement was to be with the Palestine Solidarity Campaign, but I was also an active member of the Labour Party and of Charter 88.

The latter two seemed quite reluctant to be active in any meaningful way at the time. I had phoned the chair of the Labour Party in Coventry and explained that I wanted to become a member. He seemed pleasantly surprised and was going to give my name and details to the membership secretary of my particular branch.

Some five weeks later, I phoned the secretary myself and asked: "Do you have a waiting list?" He had no idea what I was talking about, but after this things started moving.

As to activities regarding Palestine, a branch of CAABU, the Council for the Advancement of Arab British Understanding, existed in Birmingham, which met monthly in a pub in Birmingham. The usual number of participants was four or five, with a couple of them drinking heavily. The secretary distributed monthly leaflets to all the City councillors' pigeonholes and that was it. When I became somewhat critical, they suggested I improve things myself.

I found out accidentally that my grandson had a classmate whose dad, Hanna Khamis, was Palestinian and I roped him in, but it took a disastrous meeting to end any connections with Birmingham CAABU. Sarah Roy was to come and speak on behalf of CAABU in Coventry and nobody had even bothered to collect her, let alone take her to her hotel, or bring her to the meeting.

Hanna, (a co-founder of Coventry branch of Palestine Solidarity Campaign), and I decided to go it alone. Hanna with me in tow took Sarah to her hotel and drove her to the station the next morning. That was the modest start of our Palestine Solidarity Campaign.

We also had very sound advice from John Gee, who came to speak with us in Coventry. John was himself based at CAABU in London, but told us about the fairly recent start of the Palestine Solidarity Campaign (PSC), which according to him would be the truly active group on the ground. Furthermore, he also advised us to keep up our CAABU membership, since the London based founders did have some excellent speakers as well as resources. But more importantly to us, when we started inviting ourselves to speak to a variety of schools' fifth- and sixth-formers, using the name of CAABU seemed far less confrontational.

In 1988, during the first Intifada, one of the field workers from *Al Haq*, the Palestinian branch of the European Convention of Human Rights, was on a speaking tour in England.

We invited Khaled Batrawi and used the occasion as the official launch of Coventry's new PSC branch. We had very good attendance from a smallish circle of activists, but a very wide and varied list of supporters that we had built up.

I hosted Khaled that night and we had a long chat. It was Khaled who persevered in getting me to write down my own memoirs, which I did initially in sections, to fit into the quarterly bulletin called *The Olive Stone*, which was Hanna's baby.

The next morning, Khaled hummed and hawed when I suggested various breakfast possibilities, until I said, "If you weren't Muslim, I'd offer you bacon and eggs.

A wide smile spread over his face and he said, "I'd like bacon and eggs very much."

He was the third Muslim I had met who thought nothing of eating pork. One of my pupils at Queensbridge School in Birmingham used to tuck with relish into sausages saying, "I know I shouldn't, but they are really tasty." And of course Rashida thought nothing of eating pork either.

From that time on, we became very active indeed. Weekly stalls, talks to various sixth-formers – this was mainly my job, as a retired teacher – demonstrations, national events and more.

My talks, mainly to fifth- and sixth-formers but also to university students, Labour Party branch members etc., usually consisted of a short introduction, accompanied by maps and photos, after which I asked my audience to form small groups and write down anything they wished to question me about. This way I felt I wasn't talking at them, but involving them far more. It proved very successful, even with large groups of younger students.

Memories of two such occasions are still very much with me: on the first occasion, I entered what was virtually a hall with around 150 students milling about. It turned out two adjacent schools had decided to combine their fifth and sixth forms for this event. I asked them to sit anywhere suitable for them, preferably to see me or at least hear me. After my own brief introduction, which always consisted of my own background and some maps and photos, I asked them to form groups of six to seven students. Within six minutes they were to write down anything they wanted to question me on, after which I would collect their papers and answer their questions.

While they were sitting busily formulating their questions, two teachers rushed in belatedly and in panic: they had only just realised that I had been left to fend for myself with such a large number of youngsters. They heaved a sigh of relief seeing that all was well.

The second one started as a great surprise: following our usual letters of self-invitation addressed to heads of sixth forms in September, one of them, Helena Ranson, phoned me shortly after this to invite me to their school. During our conversation she revealed that she had been born in Palestine herself, daughter of a British Police Officer. This made me very wary: the British Mandatory Authorities by and large supported the Jewish settlers; would I muster enough tact to deal with the likely situation?

I need not have worried: Helena's father had previously served in India and had become radicalised to the extent that he opposed any kind of colonialism. Helena supported what I had to say and soon became a staunch supporter of our branch of PSC. She was an outstandingly progressive, broad-minded as well as sensitive person, who introduced her students to cultures as well as writings from the world over. She was something of a poet herself.

Sadly, Helena became unwell within a relatively short period of our working together and was eventually diagnosed with terminal cancer. The disease progressed so swiftly that on the Sunday shortly after entering hospital, when I phoned her husband Stewart about a convenient time to visit, he told me that she had been given between a week and ten days to live.

"Stewart, I'm teaching a class tomorrow, but I'll phone you when I finish and come straight to the hospital."

But when I phoned on Monday Stewart, sounding desperate, said: "It's too late Hanna, she's dying."

The news came as a bad shock and was quite devastating. Helena died in the early hours of the morning. Even so, she had written farewell cards to members of our group when she realised she had barely days to live. I still have mine.

The preparations for the funeral were extraordinary: Stewart, with two or three friends, invited anyone who ever had any dealings with Helena's many activities – in and outside the school – and organising everything took almost a week. My contribution during the week was to cook massive amounts of food for them, an activity I tend to escape into when I'm upset. Hanna would drive me regularly to Stewart's house to deliver full saucepans and collect the empty ones.

On the day of the funeral, which was held in a smallish church, I remember the air of great emotion and sadness but even more that of a celebration: there were contributions from students as well as from groups, and a brilliant West African Drummers' group, among other things. It was a truly memorable celebration of Helena's life. She deserved no less.

Part Four
1989–2009

This was my homeland

REMEMBER THE MARTYRS
OF PALESTINE
شهداء فلسطين
RECENTLY EIGHT MURDERED
ON SUNDAY 20ᵗ MAY 1990 __

Chapter Thirty-two

In 1989, a year following our launch of the Coventry branch of the Palestine Solidarity Campaign, and two years into the first Intifada, a women's delegation from the Socialist Movement, founded by Tony Benn, went for a fortnight to the Palestinian Occupied Territories and asked me to join them. We were known as 'Women for Socialism.'

The visit was a true eye opener for me: although I had often encountered Arab people in daily life prior to the 1948 war, I had never before been in exclusively Palestinian areas. We were based in a modest and pleasant hotel in East Jerusalem named Al-Kazar from which we travelled to different areas daily, at that time even to Gaza. There were not as yet any checkpoints although there were refugee camps, frequently surrounded by fences. Ramallah was a bustling, lively town partly very modern, as were parts of Bethlehem.

Most astounding of all was the inventiveness and positive attitude of the Palestinians: the Israeli authorities had closed universities, so lecturers gave seminars and tutorials in their homes and sometimes in their cars. Likewise, kindergartens in Jerusalem were closed (what a security risk!), but there were always back doors. One lecturer, who specialised in botanic sciences, grew masses of vegetable seedlings, which he distributed widely. And in the Gaza strip, a women's cooperative raised a herd of sheep and a ram, which were used for both meat and wool.

We also came across two quite new institutions, one the Early Childhood Resource Centre, producing various useful toys, guides on how to make such toys and books for the very young. I had met and hosted its founder/ director, Asia Habash, when she spent a couple of days in Coventry, observing the work of the international Education Development Institute, where Smadar was working at the time. Asia was an outstandingly intelligent and progressive woman, who inspired her co-workers. The books for the very young, some of them to colour and paint in, were delightful.

The other institute, dealing with slightly older children, was the Tamer Institute for Community Education. Again, they produced excellent books and had quite an input into schools. Moreover, they had come up with a scheme of reading-passports, "Ana aqra!" (I read!). Such passports were colour-coded and had some eight or ten pages each. Every time a child finished a book, he/she would write something short about it on a page. A teacher or a guide from the institute would ask them a few questions, then stamp the page and they would proceed to another page. Once all the pages were completed, they would graduate to a new passport. This was extremely popular amongst the children who lacked any official documentation. The reading-passports looked like proper passports, with the highest ranking one in maroon.

When I revisited many of these institutions in 2005, I found that, against all odds, the Early Childhood Resource Centre had branched out into numerous towns and neighbourhoods and so had the Tamer Institute.

Last but not least was the Inash Al Usra, in translation Support of the Family. Its founder, Umm Khalil, who was still alive at the time, explained to us that after the 1948 war, she found all those desperate women, mainly widows, often with children, sitting by the roadside. She started with modest tents, but succeeded with financial support from a number of sources to build up spacious dormitories as well as classes, initially often concentrating on literacy and numeracy. This developed to acquiring various skills; mainly those that could help the women make a living.

Again, by 2005, although Umm Khalil was no longer alive, the institution had grown to incorporate training for nurses, teachers, traditional Palestinian machine embroidery, hairdressers, IT tutors and more. All these are amazing, but not atypical examples of the Palestinians' summud (steadfastness).

We were also introduced to the Women in Black organisation, at the time a small voluntary Israeli group that stood weekly in front of the Israeli parliament, holding up "End the Occupation" placards. They were often cursed, spat at and generally abused by the majority of passers-by. The main coordinator of another group, which also participated in the weekly vigils, was Hava Keller of the Women's Organisation For Political Prisoners, WOFPP. This group existed to take up cases of Palestinian women, including mundane matters such as allowing families to bring warm clothing, medication and more, to lawyers representing the women in court. Hava and I quickly made friends.

From then on, every time I was about to visit the Occupied Territories I would ask her to be my official hostess prior to travelling and she always came to visit me in East Jerusalem so we could have a tasty Palestinian meal and a good chat. I admired Hava greatly, although we do not see eye to eye on every point. Hava still believes in a Jewish Democracy, whereas to me, this is a contradiction in terms. But she certainly did her full quota of hard work and more.

Women in Black regularly sent some of their members to checkpoints to ensure that as little abuse as possible took place and to use cameras when words didn't carry enough weight. By now, this has grown into a separate organisation, Machsom Watch, in translation Checkpoint Watch, of women taking turns to watch checkpoints on a daily basis, trying to intervene when guards behave roughly to Palestinians. Very frequently this would be the case.

At the end of our tour, I managed to visit Khaled and his family, and I stayed with them for a few days. Since then, I have always included them in my visits to the Palestinian Territories.

Back in Coventry, we redoubled our efforts to help the Palestinian NGOs we had made initial contact with, such as the Tamer Institute and others. They forwarded us very useful material for my school visits. Equally, since we were now on the WOFFP list, we received regular requests to write letters of protest and/or applications to the relevant authorities.

Soon after my return from the first visit to the Occupied Territories, I renounced my Israeli citizenship and paid good money for it. You are sent a document, requesting you to present it every time you enter or exit the country. I did take the document with me, just in case, but I wouldn't have dreamt of presenting it. I could have landed myself in a lot of trouble, since Israelis and even more, former Israelis, are not officially permitted to visit the Occupied Palestinian Territories.

Once I had been to the real Palestine, I felt strongly that I wanted to return at some point. However, my next visit didn't materialise until 1994, a year after the Oslo Accords were signed. Most of us felt very doubtful about them at the time, to a point that a number of people left the Palestine Solidarity Campaign altogether.

Similarly, some individual Palestinians with great foresight refused to be part of the PNA, the Palestine National Authority, notably, Edward Said and Hayder Abd el-Shafi, whom we had met on our first visit to Gaza. But mostly we felt we should at least give it a chance.

It was already becoming clear that all the Accords had achieved was to give Yassir Arafat and his clique in Tunisia an opportunity to return to the Palestinian Territories and to end their marginalisation. As to the Accords themselves, they gave little, if anything, to the Palestinians. They ended up with what was a sorry "authority" ruled by nepotism and increasingly, corruption. As long ago as 1994, many Palestinian friends told me that those accords had not brought any real improvements to their fast diminishing areas. Since then, the downward spiral has been dizzying.

Whereas the Palestinian representatives had hardly anything but vague promises, the Israelis took advantage by creating facts on the ground, i.e. grabbing more and more land and making the lives of the Palestinians increasingly harder.

Hava phoned me in on the evening of my arrival at the Al-Kazar Hotel in Jerusalem where we had previously stayed and asked whether I would like to come to a demonstration in Tel Aviv the following day. I did, and following Hava's instructions, found it quite easy to find the Cinémateque outside which the modest demonstration took place. The theme was the Nobel Prize Yitzhak Rabin had received the previous year after signing the Oslo Peace Accords with Shimon Peres and Yassir Arafat. Rabin, the "man of peace" who, when there were international complaints of the IDF shooting children who threw stones at Israeli tanks, advised the Military: "Just break their bones."

Our placards proclaimed: "The prize is here, where is the peace?" Despite our small numbers, we were shouted at and abused. The following year Rabin was assassinated in Tel Aviv by a right-wing extremist (nowadays the group the assassin belonged to is part and parcel of the establishment) during a public speech he gave.

At the end of the demonstration, Hava took me to the WOFPP office, which was just one room in a small apartment and was the hub of numerous far-reaching activities. The rest of the apartment was occupied by a lawyer who worked for WOFPP as much as she could.

Hava mentioned that the following morning would be visiting day at Tel Mond prison, roughly located between Tel Aviv and Jerusalem. Red Cross buses would take relatives to Tel Mond and return them after their visit. WOFPP were particularly anxious regarding two underage girls, 14 and 15 years old, who were being held in an adult prison.

"You can't get into the prison," said Hava, "but you can take in the surroundings and get a feel for what it's like."

"Try and stop me," was my response.

The next morning at 6 –, I was at the designated place in Nablus Road and an old rickety bus soon turned up. Meanwhile, I had met one of the girls', Najlah's, parents, and found out that three relatives were allowed on each visit, but on this occasion, neither of her siblings could make it. I immediately had an idea of how I could get into the prison: I would be the auntie from England.

We arrived at around 8am. It was still bitterly cold. The only shelter was a corrugated iron roof for which Hava's group had petitioned long and hard. There were a few benches, but not nearly enough for the waiting visitors. Somewhere there were also some very basic toilets. The whole compound had just one gate through which visitors could gain access, with the gate opening between 8 and 8.15am.

While we were waiting, Hava explained to me that Najlah and her cousin, who was a bit of a tearaway, had decided to see what prison was like. They went to the most heavily guarded gate of the Haram Ash-Sharif as it also leads to the Wailing Wall. Najlah's cousin took out her little knife and called out, "Come on, do something."

Najlah responded by brandishing her small knife. They were promptly arrested and taken to the Moskobiya, an interrogation centre, previously a Russian monastery, where they were beaten repeatedly around the head and made to sign a document in Hebrew of which they didn't understand a word.

In court, despite the testimony of an Israeli police officer, who affirmed that the girls hadn't touched anyone, they were sentenced to seven years' imprisonment for attempted murder.

It was 11am before things started moving. The first batch of visitors was allowed into a small anteroom, where we were searched. Luckily for us, Mr Abu Shusha, Najlah's father, was in the first lot to go through.

I had no problem getting in, although my camera was confiscated, but Najlah's mother was not so lucky. She had brought some schoolbooks for Najlah and they were definitely forbidden.

I cannot remember a grimmer place than the interior of the prison. It was uniformly grey since the floor, walls and even ceiling were made of cement. A dim, naked bulb was the only light. The prisoners were sitting behind a thick grille with slats so narrow that one could barely fit two fingers through.

When the guard was not near, Najlah's father slipped her a tiny pack of chewing gum, also strictly forbidden. Najlah looked thoroughly dejected and miserable.

While we were there, I also walked along the row of prisoners and counted at least four other underage girls.

On the way back, Mr Abu Shusha told me that he had a brother who was a physician living in the USA. The brother had tried to find out what Israeli law was in terms of minors. The Israeli embassy categorically denied that they had minors in prison. So what was the mystery? Israeli law was that you could only imprison 18 years old and upwards and yet they had 14 year olds in their adult prisons.

It was clarified by a Palestinian member of the authority: there is one law supposed to cater for all, but in the occupied territories, there are Military Orders which simply overturn laws as they see fit. In the case of minors in prison, the law is indeed 18 years or over, but Palestinians are deemed adults from the age of 12 onwards. When I told friends in Jerusalem and Ramallah about this, they were not in the least surprised. They were groaning under the constant Military Orders that spring up at a moment's notice.

One frequent example would be that you may want to visit your friends but the area is already closed down by a Military Order by the time you arrive.

One positive surprise during this visit happened on the day I went to Haifa to visit Mother's grave. On this occasion, I decided on the spur of the moment to have a look at my former home. Haifa had meanwhile become literally upwardly mobile, with those who could afford it moving to live on Mount Carmel. Peace Street seemed much poorer.

While I was looking, a woman came out of our former neighbour's house and called in Arabic to a young boy across the street. Instinctively I went over to her and asked her whether she was Arab. She assented and I told her that her home had originally been Arab too. Of course I had to come in. The handsome house had been subdivided into four apartments, and she told me that Peace Street as well as other parts of Haifa was completely mixed again. I was greatly cheered by this: a small step in the right direction. A lawyer explained to me later that Haifa was one of the very few places that permitted Palestinians to buy properties in Jewish neighbourhoods and, even more rare, Haifa's Israelis don't appear to mind living side by side with Arabs.

When I got back to Coventry, I wrote to all the English national papers about Najlah's case. The only ones to take it up were *The Morning Star*, minute in readership, and *The Observer*. The latter had a Middle East reporter based in Jerusalem. He phoned me in Coventry and also went to visit the Abu Shusha family. Following this, he wrote a very sharp article and it helped to the extent that Najlah was freed after 'only' one year.

In 1994, during local elections, I had resigned from the Labour – or what was fast becoming the New Labour – party. One of its MPs, Dave Nellist, was far too left wing for the new stance the party was adopting, although he had been voted MP of the year for his hard and honest work. Instead, a different MP was foisted on the constituency.

Even after I had moved to London in 1997, my own MP, who was still in Coventry, was Geoffrey Robinson, flush with money, a great friend of Blair, who tended to surround himself with the very wealthy and/or celebrities and there was no way I was voting for him. Since that time, I have never voted New Labour, unless I found myself in a marginal constituency.

Chapter Thirty-three

In September 2000 the second Intifada erupted. There had been growing tensions between Israelis and Palestinians when Ariel Sharon, the bully and instigator of murderous war crimes, bought a house in the Arab sector of the old city, which he didn't use for daily purposes, but which served as a great provocation, since he hung a great big Israeli flag from it.

Since this did not have the desired effect, he appeared with hundreds of soldiers in the compound of Haram Al-Sharif, one of the very holy Muslim sites, with hundreds of soldiers in tow, declaring he had every right to be there.

The infuriated Palestinians started throwing stones, mainly at the worshippers by the Wailing Wall and this in turn provoked police and guard response out of all proportion. This second Intifada was far more bitter than its predecessor, because it sprang out of despair and frustration. It was also the start of the infamous 'suicide bombings'.

After the first Intifada there had been some very rare occasions of young men committing suicide, but these had been private affairs, not aiming at anyone else. The new phenomenon of deliberately aiming at Israeli targets was something new and very disturbing.

Nobody remembers now that Hamas, the main perpetrators of suicide bombing, had initially been funded and
encouraged by the Israeli secret service during the first
Intifada, so as to split and weaken the PLO (Palestine Liberation
Organisation). Neither does anybody appear to think of the
original suicide bomber: the much revered, heroic, biblical
Samson, who, after being blinded and left helpless, eventually
could bear his humiliation no longer. On the occasion of a great
celebration in the amphitheatre, he was about to be brought
out for the Philistines to mock and taunt him again. Samson,
whose hair, which was the source of his strength, had grown
again and who was at the end of his endurance, prayed to
god: May my soul perish with the Philistines! He pressed hard
against the two pillars either side of him, and brought down
the amphitheatre with the whole audience and himself.

Although suicide bombing is very negative and hard to
forgive, remembering the biblical story of Samson serves as
an example of what people can be driven to resort to, once
they completely lose hope.

At some point in the late eighties, I had read about a group of
Palestinians in the satellite town of Bethlehem, Beit Sahour,
who had adopted the motto of the original founding fathers of
the USA, "No taxation without representation!" In Beit Sahour,
which boasted many carpentry workshops, this resulted in
the Israeli army going in and smashing most of them.

Once the second Intifada started, a resident of Beit Sahour,
Ghassan Andoni, an academic as well as an activist of non-
violent resistance, together with George Rishmawi, Huweida
Arraf, Adam Shapiro and Neta Golan, founded the Palestinian
Centre for Rapprochement between Peoples, Al-Markaz
Al-Flastini li'l-taqarub bein Ash-Shu'ub, and decided to try

and start a voluntary international movement to let people see what goes on in the Occupied Territories, as well as to help Palestinian farmers. Having read about it, I decided to join. Shortly after the International Solidarity Movement (ISM) was started, I went to Palestine under their guidance in winter 2001–2002.

There were about 20 of us from the UK, arriving singly, but once we cleared customs and the usual questions – "What is the purpose of your visit?" "Where will you be staying?" "Do you have Jewish friends?" – there was Ghassan waiting at the entrance to the airport with a placard directing us.

Once we had all assembled, he drove us by minibus to our base, The Three Kings Hotel in Beit Sahour, but conditions there were so grim that initially Gill, another participant, and I booked into another hotel, The Bethlehem Star, in Bethlehem itself. After a couple of days, some others from the group joined us.

For the first two days, we underwent training at The Three Kings Hotel. This was basically defensive training: an onion or a cloth soaked in vinegar against tear gas, not responding to any provocations, which parts of your body to shield and how and so on.

On the third day, we were taken to the Salfeet area, where we were based in the village of Marda. The men had more space: they were housed in a substantial house belonging to a physician who had left the country. We also had breakfast and an evening meal there. We women were accommodated in a much smaller house: seven of us in one room and eight in the other. It was bitterly cold in the houses, a small brazier in the evening providing the only source of heat, and the water was icy. Only one woman braved the elements and had a shower halfway during the week of our stay.

It certainly gave us some insight into the lives of Palestinians in the Occupied Territories, by now much worse than at that time.

Our host, a Palestinian Venezuelan, told us that when he decided to return to his country of origin, the Israeli border guards simply tore up his Venezuelan passport.

We were also shown a house where a bereaved family with a toddler lived. The widow was eight months pregnant. On one occasion, a sudden curfew had been imposed. Her husband dashed out to bring in the toddler and was promptly shot. He was bleeding heavily and his wife tried to call the ambulance repeatedly, but it wasn't allowed through and her husband bled to death on his doorstep. How would the widow with her young children survive?

Also, in Marda, we saw a demolished house: apparently the owner was a wanted man. He had left the house quite some time ago and the present residents were renting. The Israelis simply demolished the house, an event barely noteworthy in the Occupied Territories.

Our job consisted of dismantling roadblocks in various villages in the area. These were high mud barriers that stopped cars and ambulances getting in and out of villages. They were also all but impossible for pedestrians to navigate. My particular job, as well as that of another older woman, was to stop digging if we saw Israeli police/border guards and to engage them in conversation so that the Palestinian villagers could slip back safely. At 73, I was by far the oldest but still very fit.

On one occasion, we encountered some Christian Zionists from Canada. They stopped their car to approach us and to shower us with verbal abuse. To my reply that I was Jewish, their reaction was almost violent. Not long after they left, some Israeli border guards appeared. Speaking to them was much easier. But their mentality was astounding, particularly since I was talking to a highly educated young man, who was about to go to university after his service. I ventured that Hebrew and Arabic seemed to have many similarities.

"Not at all!" was his response.

"Well, the words 'Shalom' and 'Salaam' are almost the same," I argued.

"Salaam has different connotations," he claimed.

After this I made a stupid mistake.

"Oh, so you know Arabic?" I asked.

He didn't, of course.

"But how can you talk about connotations if you don't know the language?" This only served to annoy him and he stopped chatting altogether.

The third lot of visitors, who were illegal settlers, stopped their car on the main road when they saw us, jumped out and belaboured us with their fists. Luckily for us, some more or less peaceful policemen who had been waiting on the main road, intervened and pulled the men away from us, while they were still complaining, "Do something! You have uniforms. Why don't you do anything?"

Nowadays, in 2009, and for quite a few years before that, this would, of course, be quite impossible: the police would have joined the settlers and would, in all likelihood, have arrested us. Our efforts were in vain. Within a day or two, the bulldozers returned and rebuilt the roadblocks.

Once we completed our week in the Salfeet area, we were taken to Nablus (the Arabic pronunciation of the Greek Nea Polis, New City) for a relaxing weekend. We stayed in a beautiful hotel with hot water, well-furnished rooms and great Palestinian food. This time I only shared with one person, Gill. In the evening there was to be a *hafla* (party) in the courtyard and I went, throwing caution to the wind and drinking numerous delicious cups of Arabic coffee with cardamom. Guaranteed insomnia! The *hafla* consisted mainly of men sitting round tables and chatting, while consuming coffee or mint tea and eating sweetmeats.

A young *oud* player entertained the participants. I asked him whether he knew the old Bedouin song, *Ya bint Ish-Sheikh Al-Arab*. He had never heard of it, so I sang it to him:

> *Ya Bint Ish-Sheikk Al-Arab,*
> *Ma Titla'sh Al-Jabaal*
> *Liyu'kilek Al-Wahwe.*

The translation being:

> "Oh, daughter of the Arab Sheikh,
> Do not climb the mountains
> For the jackal will eat you."

The music is based on a simple, recognisably Arabic rhythm, repetitive, but not in the least dull. The variations and elaborations see to that. The *oud* player repeated the tune after me and soon started improvising on it, with me singing along and weaving the tune in and out through the instrument. He ended by thanking me profusely for something I had enjoyed so much in any case.

On Christmas Eve, which was a free day for us, I managed to smuggle myself into the Church of the Nativity, or rather, into the small ancient cellar in which a large metal star signalled the exact place of Jesus' birth. I hadn't known that you had to buy tickets well in advance to enter the church, but slipped through the cordon of Palestinian policemen unobserved.

Inside the small space it was extremely crowded, with someone approaching the star from time to time to kiss it.

A group of nuns was singing "Oh come all ye faithful" first in Italian, or Latin, then in Arabic and finally in English. I had never known the song was so long! I left before the English part was even finished.

We were planning to walk from Bethlehem, or rather Beit Sahour and its Shepherds Fields, to Jerusalem, on Christmas Day. We were a large group, headed by the scouts and, after them, various peace activists: Palestinians, Israelis who could manage to get into the Palestinian Territories via various byways and quite large numbers of internationals, the latter having increased to around eighty, mainly Italians.

Our procession was stopped halfway by a tank and Israeli soldiers in full armour facing us. There was no way we would be permitted to go to Jerusalem.

Initially we sat down on the ground while Peter, a member of our group who was a priest and an outstanding negotiator, tried his best. The only thing we achieved, after I sang some Russian songs, since I had noticed the Orthodox Russian Cross round the necks of some of the soldiers, was that they started making eye contact with us and even accepting some sweets one of our group offered them. But the official position was not changed.

"Why are you so afraid of us?" I asked one of the soldiers by the tank as we were preparing to leave.

"Believe me, we are not afraid of you," he responded.

"Well, it very much looks like it: you are here fully armed and with a tank, while we are fewer in number, completely unarmed and obviously no danger to anybody, yet you will not let us pass." He made no reply.

"We shall come again tomorrow," said Ghassan, but the following day made no difference. My last evening was spent in a restaurant in Sheikh Jarrah, a completely Arab neighbourhood, the very place that, as I write, the Israeli Authorities have just chosen for two house demolitions as a start, on the 19th of July. They are to form an extension of the illegal settlement of the adjacent Nahlat Shimon, with the aim of turning the whole neighbourhood into an entirely Jewish one.

After my return from every visit I would write up my observations and many of them appeared in article-form on various websites, while a few made their way to our English Palestine News.

It seems as if my body had never unlearned the Middle Eastern rhythms: In early 2002, a young Palestinian dancer, Maysoun Rafidee, who was on a one year scholarship at the Laban School of Dance in London, volunteered to teach a course in basic Dabke dancing, the popular Palestinian folk-dance, twice a week. During the first session Maysoun asked me where I had learned the Dabke rhythm. Similarly a friend from PSC, Hilary Wise, immediately said, "You've done this before."

I was at a loss, I hadn't done this particular dance before, but I felt at home with it. Only when I ended up in the mental ward for old people over a year later and was diagnosed, aged 76, with bipolar disorder, did I have an inkling of how and when this had happened.

✧

In summer 2003, I entered into email correspondence with Abd El-Fattah Abu Srour, Abd for short. He was the director of Ar-Rowwad (the pioneer) Youth Centre in Aida Camp, a refugee camp close to Bethlehem. They were looking for someone to teach English for a month if possible and I agreed.

I had planned to go in September 2003, but at last my bipolar condition got the better of me. This time it was not depression, but its opposite. I span out until I was no longer lucid, barricaded myself in the house and unplugged the phone. And all that because I was convinced the Israeli Secret Services were after me!

They were hacking into my computer and doctoring my television programmes. What wonderful megalomania! Megalomania being of course a well-known symptom of bipolarity, as is paranoia. Eventually, Smadar had to call the police to break the front door down and it took them about an hour and a half to persuade me to come outside, where they promptly sectioned me for 48 hours. I remember nothing of this period except being in an ambulance and being furious about it.

After a day or two, when I had regained my lucidity, a very charming young doctor sat by me and asked me to piece together what I remembered of the whole episode. She stopped me halfway through my unpacking of the ludicrous fantasy of the Israeli secret service, to say: "I think professionally I should tell you that I am Palestinian."

I sat there and forgot to close my mouth, something that happens very rarely to me. I was particularly fortunate because the doctor, Nadia Dabbagh, did a great deal for me beyond the call of duty. She also told me that Edward Said had died the previous day and we both sat in mute grief.

The condition is still with me and, although being diagnosed at 76, I was lucky in being referred to a very sympathetic outpatients department that still checks on me. I was also prescribed stabilisers, but the most important to me is the realisation that my depressive moods had not been largely caused by sloth. Nadia (now Nadia Taysir-Dabbagh) meanwhile has a post at the Tavistock Clinic and she now has a baby too.

During my stay in hospital, I also became curious about the many question marks that have accompanied me throughout my life. Which occasions elated me beyond the normal? I had known about the depressions, but was at a loss regarding their opposite.

Eventually it began to dawn on me that travelling, seeing new places and meeting new people was certainly part of it. Being curious about people and wanting to communicate with almost anyone was equally so, much to Ernest's dismay, but the main factor was, without doubt, dance, which at times, especially when I was working on the choreography of a dance-drama, had the curious effect of making me border on a manic condition.

While still in hospital, I asked Smadar to bring me the memoirs in Hebrew of my former teacher, Yardena Cohen, and they were a revelation: my love of movement, my particular affinity to the Middle Eastern rhythm which had various Palestinians ask me whence I had acquired it, all became clear from reading her beliefs, aspirations and points of view.

One of the results of my staying in hospital for five weeks was that I had to postpone my visit to Palestine. This wasn't convenient or even feasible for Abd, as it meant I would arrive in the holiday period, when some of the students were busy revising for exams, while others were preparing a play to be shown in Bethlehem. Because of this, I was somewhat superfluous. I believe I could have done various other jobs, but the organisers were not all that interested. Indeed, when I emailed them to say that I had to postpone the visit, why did Abd or any of his helpers not warn me that December is not a good time to come?

The worst aspect for me was the accommodation. I was given a room on the first floor of Abd's house, but the toilet and shower were in the basement, which for me was quite a problem. The stone stairs were unlit and difficult to negotiate.

After a few days, I contacted the Rapprochement Centre and they were very happy for me to help with translation work. I moved to the Three Kings Hotel that, although it had not changed for the better, was very close to the Rapprochement Centre and there was now a 'Man Friday' in the place who was extremely helpful and thoroughly honest. Although tensions between Muslims and Christians, like those between Jews and both Christians and Muslims, have deteriorated considerably in the past few years, Mohammed worked for the owner, who was Christian, and told me that there was no problem.

I met friends from old times again, particularly those from the Bethlehem region, ever more punctuated, as is all of the West Bank, by alien-looking settlements disrupting the natural beauty of the terraced undulating hills. The settle-ments looked like impenetrable fortresses, always on hilltops and overlooking their "enemy" population. I always felt they expressed the mindsets of their inhabitants better than words. One of my friends, Marina Barham, who had worked with the director of the Ar-Rowwad Centre, told me that although she had worked with him, she generally disliked his work and had started a group of her own some years ago.

I saw Marina's Inad group performance on Christmas Eve. It was a lovely play performed by young adults for children.

The Ar-Rowwad performance was aimed mainly at a group of Belgian tourists whom Abd had been in contact with. I believe he had his Ph.D. from a Belgian university. It was very disappointing. In the first place, the actors never acted and spoke simultaneously. They either spoke or rather declaimed standing still, or moved about the stage without any speaking at all. The movement during these scenes was supplied by film footage against the background. What's more, they kept talking about "the Jews". The Belgian tourists enjoyed the performance and at the end leapt to their feet to clap wildly, shouting, "Bravo!"

I was quite disturbed by the repeated use of "the Jews". I spoke to Abd and some of his co-workers about it. His reply was that it is used widely and does not mean much.

"It's a shame that it's used widely and it's understandable, but to proclaim it from the stage is unacceptable, sending out the wrong signal to the young actors and other young people, not to mention the audience. Why not use 'Zionists' or even 'Israelis' instead?"

Abd just shrugged his shoulders and was obviously not going to change anything.

As always, I had to visit Nader and his family. They knew that this visit had been at least in part a disappointment and Nader gave me a present of a children's CD after I told him that I had brought a children's cassette tape to Abd's little boy, which had been totally disregarded and dismantled by him. But more than this, Nader, who had some studio apartments at the base of his handsome house, offered me one of them free of charge and for any length of time I chose, for my next visit. The studios were usually let to students, often studying at the near-by Makassad Hospital.

However, during that visit and my penultimate one in autumn 2005, I observed a new and sad phenomenon: more people had started expressing resentments towards Jews in general, rather than towards Israelis/Zionists. Since my Arabic has improved a great deal, people would quite often take me for an Arab, albeit not a Palestinian, and so they talked openly about their resentment towards Jews. My reply is invariably that I am a Jew myself, although this makes me feel a freak or a cheat: In what sense am I a Jew? Had it not been for Hitler and his crazed racial classifications, would I still term myself a Jew?

During my stay in Bethlehem and Beit Sahour in 2003–2004, I came across another example of the growing tensions, which are exploited quite openly by Israel.

One evening I was in a queue behind three or four women waiting for Youssef, an excellent cook with great patience and good humour, who was busy behind the counter. I asked him something and the women started discussing whether I was an Arab or a foreigner. One of them ended the discussion by saying very firmly, an Arab. I smiled and said, a foreigner. Whereupon she gave a whole list of various nationals who were welcome,

"Everybody is welcome here," she said, "the French, the Italians, the Germans, the Greeks, all of them are welcome, except the Jews."

I smiled again and said, "I am a Jew."

They were dumbfounded until I pointed out that I object to the Israeli state and that I am not a Zionist.

Youssef, by the way, had a picture of the Madonna and child on one wall of his shop and inscriptions from the Qur'an on the opposite one.

Chapter Thirty-four

In the mid 1990s, both Smadar and Yael left Coventry, Yael to London and Smadar to Northampton. Although I visited frequently, chiefly London, I felt this was my longed-for opportunity to live in the capital, something I had always wanted, but to which Ernest had always violently objected.

I made my decision in early 1997, but finding an affordable home with decent public transport nearby wasn't easy. My nephew Peter, as well as another acquaintance drove me round and I settled on Tottenham, close to Seven Sisters tube station and even closer to Tottenham Green Leisure Centre, which boasted a swimming pool, the Marcus Garvey library and a gym.

The house I bought in Arnold Road was quite old, an Edwardian terraced house, and was in a miserable state of disrepair. I moved into it in November, but had to call in builders. The mess was such that I had move out for a month for work to commence, but even when I returned, there was still a terrible amount of dust and debris, not to mention mice. I was becoming depressed, but as spring came, I decided to throw a 70th birthday party in the new garden that had previously been a pile of rubble to fill two skips.

✧

When I first moved to London, I gorged on museums and exhibitions, to many of which I took my youngest grandson, Nico. I frequented concerts of classical and world music and I even went to dress rehearsals of operas. Visiting the Imperial War Museum, which also houses the Holocaust Exhibition, with Nico, gave me such a shock that I felt compelled to write a poem about it:

At the Holocaust Exhibition
On screen the old woman
Talks about the taunting and abuse
Of Jewish children in German schools.
I sit quietly, thinking: it wasn't always bad,
Not all of the time.
The screen cuts to a classroom,
Girls smiling shyly at the camera.
I start and stare:
I know them! They are Jutta, Renate, Inge –
My friends, then later not my friends.
I watch over and over
And stumble through the rest of the displays
In fear, as in a dream;
Who else might I encounter here?
Omi, my much loved grandma, in Terezin?
Aunts and uncles in Dachau?

But no more shocks,
Just the unnamed dead;
Poles, Jews, Roma, Russians,

Weeds Don't Perish

Trinkets and knick-knacks
Treasured by their owners and surviving them.
A testimony to man's descent into barbarity
Made worse by being tidy and methodical.

At home I look at my old class photo;
On its back, 1937 in my hand.
The year Jews were expelled from state schools.
The year we left for Palestine.

I sit next to our teacher, Herr Terne,
And I remember how in mid tirade against the filthy Jews
He would stop.
To ask, his voice so calm, so reasonable:
"But we have one exception, have we not?"

"Yes, Herr Terne. Came the prompt reply.
"And she is with us, is she not?"
"Yes, Herr Terne," the obedient chorus, yet again.

"And she's Lilo, is she not?"
"Yes, Herr Terne," thrice the shoddy lie.

As I sat numbly, staring at my desk,
I knew that I must stand and speak,
Say "I am no exception, I refuse to be!"

But I sat mutely, staring at my desk;

The stench of cowardice hanging above me
Like some greedy rat.

Was this the reason, although no excuse
That I rejected dear Herr Link
The bathing manager at the lovely pool
In Homburg, who taught me how to swim and jump
When I was barely seven
And welcomed me year after happy year
To play with me and spoil me?

But that last summer
When I went, as always,
To the pool straight after my arrival,
A sign above the entrance
Read "Jews unwelcome here."
I turned and walked away,
With Herr Link calling after me
Repeatedly, beseechingly, his voice rising.

I knew he wanted to let me in, but I rejected him.
It was a mean and petty act,
That still returns to haunt me now and then.

From London I also travelled a great deal: to Prague, to Budapest and small Greek islands, of which I searched out the quieter and more remote ones.

I had started travelling from Coventry. I went to lower Egypt for my 65th birthday, and even before that, I had been to Florence, Athens and some of the Greek islands. But it was so much easier from London.

Ever since my school days, Czechoslovakia, in particular Bohemia at the time, had featured in my mind as a place of fairly bloodless revolutions executed inadvertently with humour and at times quite comical.

I loved their defenestration tactics (throwing people out of windows) in which they seemed to be specialists. The best-known defenestration occurred in 1618. Bohemia's aristocracy rebelled when the new king of the Habsburg Empire was about to make the protestant faith illegal. Two aristocratic emissaries and their scribe were arguing with their Bohemian counterparts and the dispute ended when the Bohemians threw them out the window into the moat, which was full of horse manure. What can be more humiliating, especially to nobility, than being covered in shit?

Unfortunately this also contributed to the 30 years war.

From that time onwards, there is a lengthy history of noble but quite non-heroic events, one being the tale of *The brave soldier Schwejk* by Jářoslav Hašek, who spent the entire First World War trying in vain to find his regiment.

More recently, there were the underground Samizdat newspapers published secretly in Czechoslovakia, but smuggled out and published widely throughout Europe. Vaclav Havel, the first post-communist president to be, was one of the founders of these newspapers and an activist. In 1988 he was arrested as an anticommunist traitor and dissident. He was released but only permitted to do manual work. He had previously been a writer and a dramatist.

But the people had had enough of the particularly repressive regime. Starting on 18th November 1989 in Prague's Vaclav Square, 200,000 people demanded free elections. The crowd grew overnight to half a million. The revolution grew countrywide and Vaclav Square's numbers grew over 6 weeks I can't bear thinking of how cold it must have been with people chanting Havel na Hrad! Havel to the castle!

On the 29th of December, the communist government collapsed and Havel became the first president.

Not long after this, in 1991, I made my first visit to the city I had read so much about. I rented a small but pleasant apartment with a kitchenette, which the landlord had provided with some basic food. It was not quite in the centre, but only three or four stops by metro. One of those was Podebrad. It reminded me immediately of Irene Podebrad, who had been one of my classmates in Berlin. She was a particularly charming girl, albeit a little distant. She lived with her divorced German-Jewish Mother and rumour had it that her father was a Czech aristocrat. In this case, rumour proved to be true.

I loved Prague's Stara Mestra (old city) with its clock-tower opening at the top from which the apostles march round hourly on the hour, the old cobbled streets and, of course, the bridges over the Vltava River, most famously the Karlovy Most (Charles Bridge). These days it has mostly stalls selling their wares to the many tourists, still overlooked benignly by various saints on both sides of the bridge.

On the other end of the bridge a small restaurant na Kampa is known for its *Prazska Šunka s křenem* (Prague ham with horseradish), which tastes very moreish. From there more narrow cobbled streets twist their way towards the San Vitus Dome, which houses a fascinating art gallery.

After a fairly steep walk to the impressive castle, which is the government seat, you have a splendid view of the city with the river and all the bridges spreading out underneath. Closely behind is the Zlatna Ulička (Goldsmith's Lane) a well-preserved, cobbled little street of charming old houses.

One day I decided to have a look at the Jewish Quarter; apparently, unlike the common ghettos, its inhabitants had voluntarily chosen to live within their own community. The oldest working synagogue in Europe is located at the end of it. Some male tourists, mainly Germans, were paying for a rented kippah so as to enter, but I alerted them to the fact that a tied handkerchief would be sufficient. My goal wasn't the synagogue, which looked pretty boring, but I had been told of a permanent display of paintings, drawings and writings done by Jewish children in Terezin. I wasn't prepared for the shock of seeing not just the displays but under each one the name of the child, its date of birth and its date of death. It was the latter that was so devastating: almost all these children, aged roughly between ten and fifteen, died in 1944, at a time when Hitler's regime was already crumbling. Some of the pictures show normal family life as they had experienced it, flowers and pretty houses, others, mostly done by the older ones, had a strong sense of foreboding. It was heartbreaking and suddenly tears streamed down my face. The book I bought at the end of my visit explains that out of 15,000 Czech children who were deported to Terezin, 100 returned. The rest were sent to Auschwitz and death.

This was the most painful part of my visit. The memory of it stayed with me and probably strengthened my conviction that we need to respect all human beings, whoever they are. It also made me wish to return to Prague at some other time.

When I left, I was standing alongside many other tourists at the passport control queue. A young man in front of me who wasn't too steady on his feet stepped on me and apologised profusely. He reeked of drink.

"It doesn't matter, I don't mind," I reassured him.

We got chatting about our respective experiences in Prague and I mentioned that I was suffering from cultural indigestion. His response was, "We are suffering from a different kind of indigestion. We used to see the prostitutes on the way home from work in the morning." He then invited me to join their group upstairs after the check in. As soon as I arrived upstairs, which consisted mainly of a large bar, the group organiser, a young man of Punjabi descent, asked me anxiously, "What's the problem?"

"There isn't a problem." I replied, "One of your group invited me to join you."

After that, I had a hard time not to accept all the booze that was pressed on me. I eventually agreed to one spritzer and made it last until we had to go to the departure lounge. It turned out that the young men had been on a stag weekend and they had certainly made the most of it. The bridegroom's friends were mainly of Punjabi descent and that of the bride were Irish.

The departure lounge consisted of two adjoining open halls. My new friends were in the further one, while I was in the nearer one. I heard shouting and harsh reproach from a woman and the lad's response, a pitying and slightly mocking, AHaaah! More shouting and then two Czech guards appeared and hauled the lads away. I jumped up.

"They haven't done anything!" I shouted.

A woman opposite me said sternly, "They are drunk and the little girl is crying."

236

But once we were on board, in good old Czech fashion the guards reappeared with the lads in tow and let them board the plane, albeit in the back. I passed them as I went to the toilet and a couple of them thanked me for trying to defend them.

"Are you going to carry on drinking when we get back to England?"

They were indeed, until the wedding in a day's time.

"Well, full marks for stamina," I joked.

At Gatwick, while we were waiting for our luggage, the woman was next to me, as well as some of the tipsy lads.

"You see," she reproached them," you just don't think of the damage you cause."

This was too much! I turned to her furiously.

"It is you who cause damage with your shouting and hectoring. That little girl cried because you frightened her with your loud and angry shouting, not that of the young men."

She stared at me and her hen-pecked husband smiled broadly.

My second visit to Prague followed an offer in the *Guardian* newspaper and had a guide who took us on an initial tour, after which we were left more or less to our own devices. I re-visited some of the places I had seen before, but on this occasion, I also managed to find Dvořak's house. It was almost empty of visitors, with the furnishings much as they were in his time and there were some cassette tapes and CDs at what seemed to be ridiculously low prices.

During this visit I decided to go and see Terezin/ Theresienstadt, the concentration camp in which Omi had died. I took an early morning bus. It was early autumn and the weather was uncharacteristically overcast and grey. Hardly anybody was around, but, as I walked down the main street, I came across a large group of people listening to a guide who spoke fluent English. She explained how the camp was seemingly humane; how the Red Cross was allowed to visit regularly and approved of what they were shown. What they didn't see was that camp inhabitants were regularly transported hence to Auschwitz, nor what daily life in Terezin was really like.

After a while, people dispersed and only three Jewish Americans who had paid for the private guide remained.

"Which group are you with, lady?" their guide enquired.

"I'm not with any group. I came because my grandmother died here," I explained.

"Just join us," she said.

Our guide asked where Omi was transported from and, when I told her, she explained that elderly people had not been transported further, but left to die in Terezin, especially those whose husbands had served in the German army. They were also sent relatively late. I knew that Omi had been sent in autumn 1942. According to the guide, prior to being transported, they were told that were they to agree to move to Terezin, their circumstances would be much better than in Germany. They would be among their own people and would be free to do as they liked. They only had to turn over whatever they still possessed to pay for the trip.

Upon arrival, they were put into old people's homes, now dismantled. There were no beds, just straw mattresses, no heating, no medicines and very little food. Omi only survived in the camp for a few months. They were treated basically like Gazan inhabitants these days. Our guide, herself Jewish, took us to the 'factory'. In reality it was a crematorium dressed up as a factory so as not to arouse suspicion amongst the locals

– quite apart from Theresienstadt, there were numerous villages nearby.

The Germans also used the furnace, fired to a much higher temperature, to manufacture glass. Thus the smell of burning corpses was disguised.

Out of the blue our guide challenged us to identify a highly Eurocentric quotation that had been written by a Jew.

"Who wrote this: '*Oriental despotism restrained the human mind within the smallest possible compass. Asian society has no history at all, at least no known history but the history of the successive intruders who founded their empires on the passive basis of that unresisting and unchanging society*'?"

"Marx?" I hazarded.

It was.

"I don't wish to offend you, but Israel's attitude to Palestinians these days is very similar," I commented.

"I agree with you completely," she replied, but the three Americans were fuming.

"You've got to look after your own first," was their main argument.

I shut up when it became evident that they were not open to rational discussion. Shortly after this, I had to leave to catch the bus back to Prague.

"I'll give you a lift," the guide said.

In view of the paying Americans, who by now wouldn't even look at me and maintained an icy silence, I wasn't at all certain.

"Are you sure?"

"Of course I am, I'm driving that way anyway."

"But..."

"Just hop in, it's not a problem."

As we were driving off, she laughed. "You are not a proper Israeli at all," she said, "an Israeli would have said, 'Are you going that way? I'm coming.'"

The Terezin archives were closed as it was Sunday, but one of the other tourists on this visit, participating in the special *Guardian* readers' offer, was an Englishwoman living in Israel. She undertook to look up all the details in a place called Terezin House in Israel.

Not long after this I received a photocopy, which initially baffled me. With meticulous German thoroughness, all the details were there: year and place of birth, maiden name, married name, date and number of transport, date of death and cause of death. Everything was methodically noted, except the cause of death. That was left blank. Omi only survived in the camp for six months. She must have lost the will to live, for which no category exists.

Of all our relatives, only one survived, Hanne, a niece of my grandmother. She came to Israel and stayed for a short time, but then moved to the USA and married someone there.

It was in London that I heard Miriam Makeba live for the first time, as well as the Hungarian group, Muzsikas. I had initially heard them on Radio Three and was completely enchanted. When they appeared in London of course I had to go.

"Mother going to listen to Hungarian music?" said Smadar, "that can't be right."

It's true that for years I didn't want to know about anything Hungarian, but it was mainly Muzsikas who helped me realise how silly it is to dislike a whole country and its culture just because you couldn't stand your father who had originated from it. Without this group, I doubt that I would have visited Budapest at all.

In June 2001 I went for a long weekend to the city, without realising beforehand that it was the 10th anniversary of the Soviet troops leaving Hungary. Celebrations went on throughout the country. I concentrated on folk music, much of it free at open-air venues. But even here, Zionism raised its ugly head.

One evening I attended a folkloric group performance. I had a very good seat, but when the attendant asked the group of people, one of whom had occupied my seat, to move, they crossly refused.

"We asked for the best seats and this is where we are," they said.

After the attendant explained it was only the question of moving one seat, they grudgingly moved. During the interval, we started talking a little and it turned out that one couple were Israelis. The husband started speaking Hebrew and wanted to know where I had lived and been educated.

"I grew up in Haifa and went to Hugim School."

"Well, they didn't educate you very well!"

"What do you mean?" I asked, although I already knew.

The reason, of course, was that I no longer lived in Israel, neither had I any plans to leave Britain. My reply, that I had been educated in a true humanistic, rather than in a nationalistic way and was grateful for it, infuriated him. I was saved by the bell announcing the end of the interval, but he took care to change seats with one woman so he was no longer next to me.

Buda was probably the more beautiful side of the city, which had merged with Pest relatively late, in 1873. It had the most historical sites, the old castle and the St. Matthias Church, 700 years old. Unfortunately, Bartok's house in Buda was closed for renovations, but I managed to visit Kodaly's house in Pest, where much of the interior is still as it was during his life. It was also within walking distance of my delightful pension, which used to be a journalists' and writers' club with some accommodation. It included a very generous breakfast buffet, facilities for coffee and tea making in our rooms, and two buildings away, at the corner of the street, a great and modestly priced restaurant. And I loved the underground, with the short bar of music that had the typical Hungarian syncope being played at every stop.

The city boasted of numerous fascinating places inviting exploration, such as the Ethnographic Museum, the various churches, bridges and Margit Island, not to mention the famous Gellert Hotel and the many outdoor as well as indoor swimming pools, supposedly with various curative powers. Hungarians use these widely for sitting in the water to play card games and chess. I had heard of this strange practice before, but seeing it was something quite different and to me amusing.

On my last day I went to visit Margit Island. The flight was at 8pm and I had asked for the driver of the minibus to collect me at 6pm, so as to give myself plenty of time to thank the manageress and bid farewell to some of the other guests in the pension whose acquaintance I had made. The Budapest airport minibus was a great institution that enabled people to be collected from and returned to the airport at specified times, at very modest fares. It was particularly useful for tourists with heavy loads of baggage.

When I arrived at the pension, the driver, who was waiting impatiently, shooed me into the empty minibus and drove like the clappers. What was the matter with him? When I came to departures, an attendant summoned me curtly.

"But this is First Class," I protested.

"Not important," she snapped, labelled my suitcase and told me I would travel First Class.

"Why?" I asked.

"The plane is full," she said curtly, then told me to go immediately to the departure gate.

What had happened to the famed Hungarian courtesy I had experienced? All was revealed when I arrived at the gate. A sign above displayed the information that the plane was delayed by one hour, leaving at 19.00 rather than 18.00. Finally the penny dropped: my genius for numbers had failed me yet again! After digesting the fact that I had been very lucky, I walked up and down like many of the other tourists and wondered aloud why the plane was so late. Really, things should be organised better, I grumbled.

For me, amongst Central European capitals, Budapest comes a close second to Prague.

Back in London, the highlight of my return came shortly after it: the Takazs Quartet and the Muzsikas group appeared together at the Festival Hall. I had wrongly imagined that one part of the programme would be the quartet before the interval and Muzsikas after or vice versa. Instead, they interwove the music, with the quartet at times playing a part of Bartok's composition and Muzsikas taking over the tune; likewise Muzsikas, one of whose main interests was the retrieving of Bartok's original discoveries of Transylvanian and Hungarian folk music, on which he had based numerous classical compositions, would at times start a theme, which the quartet continued. And of course, sometimes, they would play in unison. Sheer magic!

I did not let the grass grow under my feet and took up Nader's generous offer in September 2005.

During this, what I imagined would be my last, visit to the Palestinian Territories in 2005, I was based in a studio flat at the ever generous and hospitable home of Nader Mahmood and his family in East Jerusalem. Tensions between Christians, Muslims and Jews had deteriorated further, no doubt fostered by the Israeli authorities, although this did not and still does not apply to the educated strata of Palestinian society. On one occasion, as I was walking along Salah-Ad-Deen (Saladin) Street, a middle aged, sour faced woman stopped me.

"Do you speak English?" she asked.

When I assented, she said, "Be careful of the Muslims round here. They are all thieves. They'll rob you and could even kill you!"

"You are speaking about my friends. I am staying with them and they are outstandingly generous and hospitable, as are other Muslim friends of mine in Ramallah and other places. How dare you denigrate people you don't even know?"

She walked away, her face as sour and bitter as before.

More saddening was the case of a little girl from the neighbourhood who used to observe me as I walked down and up the steep Al-Mutanabbi Street, often laden with food on my way up. She must have been about six or seven years old, almost always in school uniform. One day she approached me to ask, "*Inti Muslimiya?*" (Are you Muslim?)

"*La, ana mish muslimiyah.*" (No, I 'm not Muslim)

"*Inti Massihiyah,*" (you are Christian), she stated.

"No, I'm neither Muslim nor Christian."

The little girl looked confused and kept asking me. I had to be one or the other. She couldn't imagine another religion.

Eventually I took over, "*Ana mish Muslimiyah wa mish Massihiya. Meen ana, shu ana?* " (I'm neither Muslim nor Christian. Who am I? What am I?)

She looked even more bewildered.

"*Ana Yahoodiyah,*"(I'm Jewish,) I told her.

She gaped at me: was I having her on? I evidently didn't fit the image she had of Jews, or rather Israelis.

Out of curiosity, I decided to venture into West Jerusalem on one of the days. In a jewellery shop in what has become a wide pedestrian mall with the obligatory enormous McDonalds, I asked to look at the telephone directory.

I found the Saragustis' name and the shopkeepers were happy to let me phone and even refused payment, possibly because they themselves, being Mizrahi Jews, had realised I had non-European friends, a rarity in Israeli racist hierarchy. It was a real surprise to Rachel and Hayeem and of course I had to come to see them, still living in the German colony. Now retired, they seemed to enjoy a good pension, which they have used to improve their house and garden beyond recognition, as well as travelling extensively. Anat, Smadar's former kinder-garten friend, was on holiday with her daughter, travelling through Canada.

On this occasion I also looked for Yardena's name in the directory and to my great surprise, I found her number. I phoned her and she invited me to come and see her in Haifa, where she lived in a retirement home on Mount Carmel, quite close to my former school, Hugim.

Yardena had a very pleasant apartment in the retirement home, which was also next door to a hospital. When I came to see her, she was even smaller than she used to be, a shrunken little bird with a hooked nose, but with all her wits about her. She was still speaking about the need to build bridges between Arabs and Jews, in her case still in terms of dance. At the time, she was 95 years old. I have no idea whether she is still alive, but it was lovely to meet with her and reminisce about past experiences and students.

The widespread racism in Israel itself has become rather worse than when I lived there: Ethiopians are regarded only as only marginally above Arabs. Mizrahi Jews, including not only those from Arab countries, but Indians, Yemenis and North Africans, are slightly above, with Sephardi Jews at the second rung of the ladder. And of course European Jews, the founders of Zionism, by and large run the country and make practically all the important decisions.

This is manifest as soon as you arrive at Tel Aviv: the new airport terminal, a splendidly designed and quite luxurious building in which all the cleaners, sweepers and toilet assistants are black, whereas shop assistants, security personnel and of course flight attendants are white. Needless to say, starting at the airport and continuing into all of Israel you could be forgiven for assuming that the official language is Hebrew, but that English is also spoken. In theory, Israel has two languages officially, Hebrew and Arabic.

Conditions for Palestinians had worsened considerably yet again, particularly with the horrendous wall. I came up against it when I went to visit Amal Nassar, daughter of the founder of *Tents of Nations* in Beit Sahour. Initially I had met Amal when she was on a speaking tour in Britain. Jean Churm, an activist from the Palestine Solidarity Campaign, had asked me to come and speak as well. I was truly pleased by the way the chair, a postgraduate student at York University introduced us: "We are three Palestinians," he said, "I am Muslim, Amal is Christian and Hanna is Jewish."

Amal was also encouraging people to buy olive trees, a snip at £5 a tree. This was to replace the many olive trees the Israeli Occupation Force had destroyed. The *Tents of Nations* was the brainchild of her deceased father: there were numerous spacious caves on his land and he decided to invite young people from around the world to come during their holidays and learn how to respect others and live together in harmony. The family has ownership documents from Ottoman times of their lands, but even so, they have endless court cases against them because the Israelis want to take it.

We went to Amal's house and her brother showed me computer images of their project to continue their father's work, while her Mother prepared a very nice meal for us. But – wherever you sit in the house – you are confronted by the obscene wall that obscures any other view.

During this visit to Palestine/Israel I met with Dawoud Badr, director of ADRID, the Association for the Defence of the Rights of Internally Displaced Persons in Israel. The meeting was facilitated by the organiser of *Zochrot* (remembering), a small Israeli group trying to preserve the real history of Palestine/Israel. Dawoud drove me to what used to be his village, now only large boulders and a half ruined mosque with barbed wire surrounding it. He explained that in 1948, prior to the Haganah approaching the village, the elders made an agreement with the commander: the villagers wouldn't put up any fight and in return would be left alone. When the Haganah approached, the elders put up a white flag on the minaret, but this commander claimed never to have heard about any agreement. They expelled the inhabitants and razed the village to the ground, leaving only the damaged mosque standing.

I walked over some of the boulders and in between cacti, while Dawoud explained that the men would still gather for Friday prayers, initially in the mosque, then, when the Israeli local authorities of Western Galilee declared the building unsafe and would not give permission to repair it, outside. But even this was not permissible. The authorities surrounded the structure with barbed wire. Apparently, there are numerous such ruined villages in Israel, with the inhabitants or their descendants living inside Israel, but prohibited from rebuilding the ruins of their former villages. They have now formed the ADRID network, which incorporates sixteen such villages, to coordinate their efforts, with headquarters in Nazareth. So far, there have been no positive results. I didn't quite feel I could ask him about the better known Adalah organisation, which seems to have the same aims, with offices in Nazareth too.

During my 2005 stay, I also interviewed Mordechai Vanunu, who at the time was staying at the St George Hostel. He had been discharged after eighteen years in prison; the first 11 of them in solitary confinement. Initially, after having been kidnapped from London in 1988 and brought before a court in Tel Aviv, the judge asked: "I hear you have converted to Christianity?" When Vanunu assented, the judge said: "That makes you a traitor already."

My special interest was why he had converted to the Church of England. According to Mordechai, this was the only religion he had any contact with at the time. He told me he was not very convinced of any afterlife. During our conversation, I gathered that he came from a particularly orthodox family, and that for him just to become an atheist was not a viable option. His release sounds more like a house arrest: he cannot leave the country, which is his dearest wish, has to report to the police regularly and is forbidden to speak to foreign journalists. And this at a time when knowledge of Israel's enormous nuclear stockpile is common knowledge, not even denied by Israel.

During this visit I also interviewed Abu Khaled (Mohammed Batrawi), whom I had met and admired before. His story is typical of many Palestinians. The family originated from Isdood, now Ashdot, in the south. In 1948, he became separated from his family. Many of Isdood's inhabitants did not want to become refugees and remained in their homes. When the Israeli army occupied the town, they imprisoned the young men as war prisoners – precisely those who didn't want to fight in the first place. The prisoners were sent to Israeli prisons, whereas the women, elderly and children were driven to Gaza, at the time under Egyptian rule.

In 1949 Abu Khaled was released to East Jerusalem, at the time under Jordanian control. He managed to smuggle himself to Gaza. He was a thorn in the Egyptians' flesh, involved actively in trying to free the Gaza strip from Egyptian rule, not to mention being a member (later chair) of the Communist Party. As a result, he was repeatedly imprisoned till he left for Jordan via Israel. The Jordanian Authorities, however, were no different from Egypt when it came to freedom of speech and expression, and so he became well acquainted with Jordanian prisons too. Eventually he left for Kuwait. In 1959 he was deported back to Palestine and settled in Ramallah with his wife, where he still lives.

Abu Khaled studied accountancy, 'to earn my living,' he explained. His real interest had always been literature and specifically literary criticism. He became the editor of the most progressive Palestinian Newspaper and the foremost literary critic in Palestine, as well as chair of the Communist Party. I found him a most intelligent and unassuming person, gently spoken and always courteous.

My initial decision to make my 2005 visit to Palestine a farewell one was somewhat premature. It was the increasingly dire news, in large part following the election of Hamas, which urged me to see for myself. Not many people remember that it was the Israeli Secret Services who, during the first Intifada, surreptitiously encouraged and partly funded Hamas, a tiny splinter movement at that time, so as to weaken Fatah as well as more socialist movements that were functioning in a truly democratic way during that time. The Oslo Accords put paid to all that.

I also felt for the first time that I was physically ageing and that I would soon be unable to travel long distances. I had already been hospitalised twice and I felt my strength ebbing. Finally, I gave in to my longings and went again in July 2008, much against Smadar's urging "It isn't sensible, mummy."

And in various ways, it wasn't. I could no longer stay at Nader's house, as Al-Mutannabi Street leading to it was way too steep and had been difficult to manage even in 2005, I had to use taxis a great deal more than previously, but the experience of the last visit is deeply etched in my memory: both the warmth and friendship, as well as the incredible hatred, the latter exclusively from Israelis.

Nader and his family, now with four children, since Iman has given birth to twins, cooked wonderful and elaborate meals for me. He also gave me cuttings of their mint and sage, both of which are much more aromatic than the British ones. I smuggled them out in a little box wrapped in moist cotton wool. The mint survived and is now flourishing in my garden, but the sage died. Khaled and Reema in Ramallah, where I stayed the night, spoiled me just as much. But I am saddened that Khaled has long since stopped participating in any political activities. They own a beautiful house and garden and both earn very well. He is a civil engineer and she is a dentist. But his initial idealism seems to have wilted.

They have two teenage daughters and one younger son and one of the daughters made me give her a list of good universities in Britain: she was preparing to come and study in this country.

This was also the second time I inadvertently met Khaled's father, Mohammed Batrawi. Mr Batrawi, who is about my age, told me that he had now retired. He was living with his wife and friend/housekeeper, Maral Quttinieh's mother, in modest comfort.

Maral, whom I had initially met by chance on a London tube acting as a guide to a group of young Palestinian visitors – I had guessed from their conversation and idioms that they were Palestinians – had enthused greatly about Abu Khaled. She was studying journalism in France and is now a journalist in Ramallah. We met numerous times since that first time. It never ceases to amaze me how Palestinians with their horrendous difficulties still manage to look forward and keep their optimism.

The heartbreaking fact is that the situation for the Palestinians has been worsening with each visit. The *summud* of people is amazing: just surviving from one day to the next had become a resistance in itself, despite Israel's best efforts to make life as intolerable as possible for the Palestinians, so that they would just leave and disappear.

Abu Khaled, whom I met again inadvertently (this time someone mistakenly gave me a lift to his house when I was about to go to Khaled's) was a great deal gloomier about the situation. Not wanting to be rude, I suggested, "Maybe some of the leadership is corrupt."

"They are all corrupt!" he said.

His view of the future was dim, except perhaps in the long term. Within the short interval of three years between visits to Palestine, checkpoints had sprung up inside Palestinian areas. The checkpoint between East Jerusalem and Ramallah was staffed by three particularly rude and rough guards. They hauled everyone off the bus and then shouted "*Ahora!*" which means "backwards" in Hebrew.

I responded by my usual "Pardon?"

"Go back,' one said to me.

"Why?"

"Do you have a passport?"

"I do," and I presented my passport.

"You can go back and sit in the bus," she said.

"I'll wait," I said.

Both guards persevered in trying to get me to sit in the bus.

"What's your problem, lady?"

To which I would reply repeatedly, "*You* are my problem. Why are you treating me differently from the rest? Why don't you let everybody sit in the bus and you come to check our IDs inside?"

The guards became more and more furious with me. Eventually, when everyone was back on the bus, the younger guard, her face contorted with fury, all but screamed at me, "I'm doing my job!"

As the bus started to move, I called out to her, "When the SA and SS officers were brought to justice at the end of World War Two, their response was exactly the same, '*We were just doing our job!*'"

Another innovation was that of permits. Previously, I often met friends from places close to Jerusalem by the Damascus Gate. This time it was no longer possible. Marina and her group had just gone abroad and, when her Mother wanted to meet, as we had done numerous times before, I suggested, "Why don't we meet by the Damascus Gate?"

"Hanna, I can't. I haven't got a permit to enter Jerusalem. You need permits now."

Eventually, I went to her house in Beit Jala and she told me that, although Beit Jala is almost a satellite town of Jerusalem, it is now very difficult for Palestinians to obtain permits. People have become prisoners in their own homes and small towns.

Inside the Damascus Gate, an area which is until today almost entirely Arab, I observed an Israeli soldier poking his gun into an open vegetable sack belonging to a *fallahiya*, who sat behind it. I jumped up from my seat in a local cafe where I was having a drink, and rushed to confront him.

"Why are you messing with her greens?" I asked.

"She may well have a small bomb stashed away in there."

A ludicrous idea, seeing that she must have passed a whole lot of checkpoints to get to Jerusalem in the first place.

"But all this area is completely Arab," I protested, "If they don't complain, why do you intervene?

His reply was staggering, "All this is mine, everything here is mine and I can do exactly as I want."

I told him that this made him a fascist, which didn't bother him much.

"Okay, so I'm a fascist," he shrugged.

Another soldier, also in the old city, explained to me that the term "polite" does not exist in their vocabulary.

The most hate-filled person I encountered was an Israeli taxi driver originally from Morocco. On this occasion, we were speaking Hebrew. I asked him to take me to the Damascus Gate. As he was driving along, he asked, "And may I ask what business the lady has by the Damascus Gate?"

Stupidly, I fell into the trap. Instead of telling him either to mind his own business or whether he asked all his customers why they were going anywhere, I responded with, "The Damascus Gate is close to the Palestinian bus station and I am going to visit friends in Ramallah."

That set him off. He was spluttering with rage, "These people, they come and settle on our land…"

He was speaking about the Palestinians. It revealed a frightening insight into the historiography Israeli children are taught at school and most of them absorb without questioning.

But there were other meetings and events to counter this virulent hatred, which I experienced mostly in Jerusalem. I visited Hava in her apartment in Tel Aviv, after years of her coming to meet me in Jerusalem, because she knew I didn't like to go much into Israel. She has a devoted husband also around 80 years old, who immediately brought us cold drinks and later insisted I stay for lunch. Hava's words regarding the political situation were, "If in future, the next generation will ask us 'and what did you do during these years?' – all we can say is 'we tried.' "

The last four days I spent in Haifa, my hometown. After my experiences in Jerusalem and the West Bank, it turned out to be an oasis of calm. There is a great deal of mixing, and not just down-town, where I stayed in a Catholic Convent with a guest-house run by the Rosary Sisters and welcoming Christians, Jews, Muslims, Bahais and others. On the first day, I took a bus from a stop not far from my former home and walked along the street at right angles with Sha'aria As-Salaam/Rehov Ha Shalom/Peace Street. On the way, I checked with a small group of people sitting by their front step whether I was on the right track to my street. I was and of course I had to have some tea and a lengthy chat with them. They told me that they were Bedouin, although all of them wore modern dress. I didn't quite dare ask where they came from and why. It may well have been the Mount Carmel encampment, where my swearing-in ceremony to the Haganah occurred all those years ago.

And my old street was still the same. I walked all the way down it, hearing Arabic and Hebrew around me in equal measure and walked along Herzl Street, the former heart of Hadar Hacarmel and the main Shopping and Business Street. It has declined, but still is a shopping area, albeit with mostly tatty wares.

I even managed to swim in my beloved Mediterranean Sea, but got stung badly by a jellyfish. It was on the beach that I met a young couple of Mizrahi Israelis. The young man in particular had doubts and was confused and disturbed about his identity in Israeli society, neither did he go along with the established denigration of the Palestinians inside Israel. We had a long chat and I did my best to encourage him to follow his own conscience and logic: Israel is in Asia, not Europe, and

Mizrahis, like Palestinians inside Israel, could potentially live in harmony and peace. We parted on very warm and friendly terms, the young man insisting on carrying the plastic chair I had borrowed from the nearby café. When we parted, the young man bent over and, to my delighted surprise, kissed my hand! The only hand kisses I had previously experienced had been exclusively from Poles. Throughout my visit, I felt great sadness knowing that this really was the last time, yet I knew that had I not gone, I would have regretted it for the rest of my life.

Afterword

January 2009

Gaza. Operation Cast Lead. The echo of these words sends shockwaves round the whole world. The Gaza Atrocities, proclaiming Israel's shameless inhumanity more loudly, nay boastfully, than anything that had happened to date, have torn any shred of conscience and justice from Israel's self image of a civilised, progressive state. Inflicting the most horrendous suffering on the people of Gaza, murdering with impunity and blocking humanitarian aid from entering the Gaza Strip show the depths of brutality and barbarity that the country and most of its inhabitants have sunk into.

Prime Minister Olmert declared the attack a victory. A victory over whom? Over a helpless occupied and imprisoned population by their occupier.

The facts speak for themselves: According to Palestinian Medical Services during three weeks 1,300 Palestinians were murdered, 430 of them children, not to mention over 5,000 wounded. Thousands of Gazans have been made homeless thanks to Israeli tanks and bulldozers ploughing their way serenely through whole streets and neighbourhoods.

According to Israeli official figures ten military personnel and three civilians were killed.

And so Israel does not see the need for any investigation, even casting aside the report of the much esteemed judge Richard Goldstone, himself a Zionist Jew: Palestinians don't count or at best are collateral damage. The bombing of a kindergarten and the killing of its teacher in front of her charges, huddled together in terror, is targeted, as are many other deaths. There is nothing collateral about it, neither is the deliberate destruction of whole neighbourhoods.

Equally, the Israeli claim that Hamas operatives are hiding amongst the civilian population does not wash either: in most countries, and certainly in Israel, military headquarters are located in the heart of the city and soldiers on leave stay with their families in cities and villages.

What achievements can Olmert boast of? Freeing the captured soldier Gilead Shalit, a stated aim of the attack, foreseeably failed since Israel refuses on principle to talk to Hamas, who have repeatedly advocated an exchange of prisoners.

Sadly most Israelis are still blind to their state's crimes against humanity as well as war crimes. It was sickening to watch on BBC young Israelis with flags lining the streets, jumping up and down for joy and shouting, "Well done, IDF!" at the end of Operation Cast Lead.

Israel's standing in the world has plummeted. The great powers that be still do not dare condemn Israel outright, but at grassroots level there has been a wide-spread awakening leading to a marked increase of organisations, faith-based groups and individuals who have started to participate in the BDS (Boycott, Disinvestment, Sanctions) movement. And latterly flotillas loaded with humanitarian aid have started to try to reach the shores of Gaza and to break the siege. So far their mission has been thwarted by Israeli marines who have rammed them in international waters, dragged the activists to their boats by force and imprisoned them prior to releasing them to be sent back to their respective countries.

But the boats keep coming. I believe this grassroots movement is unstoppable and will eventually prevail, as it did in South Africa.

Despite the shameful silence of the world's powers I believe and hope that Operation Cast Lead may be a Pyrrhic victory. It could be a turning point: Israel may soon no longer be able to act with impunity, while no one dare speak out against it. But how much more bloodshed, how much more suffering will it take?

It is often hard not to give in to hopelessness, but I shall try to hold on to the words of the late Raymond Williams:

"To be truly radical is to believe in the possibility of good rather than the inevitability of evil."

Berlin, c.1930

First day at school, April 1933

With my mother in Berlin, c.1937

Last day at school in Berlin, April 1937

My mother said: "Did you have to sit there?" I am directly under Hitler

My wedding, 01.10.1952

Wedding, 1952

My parents are next to me and Ernest's next to him

Just practising
Jerusalem, c.1956

First time in England
Bristol, 1954

Jerusalem, not long before we left for good
c.1957

Holiday in St. Mawes, Cornwall
On the top of the old castle

Birmingham Minorities – learning a Ghanaian dance

Practising the Ghanaian dance

With my class at the Steward Centre for Young Immigrants (c.1979)
I am top right

At the Steward Centre for Young Immigrants
c.1979

The Victoria Falls
Locally known in Shona as "the Rain that Thunders"

With some of my pupils on sports day
Highfield Highschool

Second year at the co-op.
We were eventually allowed to help a bit
Here – planting seedlings

On holiday from Zimbabwe, Christmas
1983 (their summer)

Not surprisingly at nursery school my
grandson announced that his grandmother
is black, like most Africans.

First grandson

April 1981

Voluntary teaching in the holidays
A cooperative of former freedom fighters in the South. The first year there, 1983
We still taught by candlelight

Caribbean dance

My farewell to the Birmingham Minorities dance group before going to ZImbabwe
Winter 1981–2

One World Week evening:
A festival with various groups
Here the Banghra dancers have just jumped down from the stage

We are all Banghra dancers!

At break, talking with the Nigerians

Birmingham One World Week
Our Minorities dance group ran a workshop in the afternoon

1989

Vigil on the steps of Coventry Cathedral

1994 – No problem at that time with going to Jericho, which was completely Palestinian then

Excavations were going on.

1994 – Entrance to the Museum of Islamic (Palestinian) Art

Haram Ash-Sharif: Photos of martyrs from the first Intifada

Damascus Gate 1994

Quite unadorned and not 'modernised' as it is now

July 1989, first Intifada, north of Gaza city

Tent given to family after house demolition – common occurrence

Afro-American-Jewish band

Israel wanted to re-convert them, so they founded their own village and have nothing to do with the state; at least not officially

During my ISM (International Solidarity Movement) stay

With the ISM, 2001–2
I had to go and chat to soldiers if they approached
On the back of the photo are the words:
"5 feet woman terrifies Israeli soldier!!!
Sorry Hana – for saying you were 4' 11" – Hélen"

'In front of my home in England, autumn 2009'